Mark Duran–Greyhound

OVER THE HILL

BUT NOT OUT TO LUNCH! *OVER 40 AND STILL COOKIN'*

By Lloyd Kahn, Jr.

Edited by Marianne Orina
and Daniel Rogoff

Book Design by David Wills

SHELTER
PUBLICATIONS INC.
PO BOX 279 BOLINAS CALIFORNIA 94924

Distributed in the United States and in Canada
by The Body Press, a division of HPBooks, Inc.

Library of Congress Cataloging-in-Publication Data

Kahn, Lloyd.
Over the Hill But Not Out to Lunch!

1. Physical fitness–United States–Miscellanea.
2. Middle age–United States–Attitudes–Miscellanea.
I. Orina, Marianne. II. Rogoff, Daniel. III. Title.
GV510.U5K34 1985 613.7'0973 85-25101
ISBN 0-936070-05-6 (pbk.)
ISBN 0-89586-457-6 (The Body Press)
68452

10 9 8 7 6 5 4 3 2 1

First printing: November 1985

Printed in the United States of America

Shelter Publications, Inc.
P.O. Box 279
Bolinas, California 94924 USA

The photo on the first page of the book is of Annabel Marsh and Caroline Merrill on their run across America in 1984. (See p. 84.) The photo on the opposite page is of Leo Le Bon (see p. 71) on a rock climbing trip.

Many of the photographs were from scrapbooks and private collections. We have given credit whenever possible.

CREDITS

Tape Transcribing & Typesetting
Trudy Renggli
Barrie Stebbings

Production Manager
Marianne Orina

Assistant to the Art Director
Patricia Maloney

Production Art & Pasteup
Patricia Maloney
Belinda Zell
Ian Gaffney

Public Relations
Daniel Rogoff

Cover Art
Design by David Wills
Photo-Montage by Gary Fox
Hand Tinting by Sally Wetherby

Display Type
Sara Schrom, TBD
San Rafael, California

Typefaces
Text: Press Roman
Headlines: Goudy Extra Bold
Pull Quotes: Goudy Bold Italic

Typesetting Done On
IBM Electronic Selectric Composer
run by Pilara 2000 Word Processor

Photo Printing
General Graphic Services
San Francisco, California

Photostats
Marinstat
Mill Valley, California

Color Separations, Cover
Focus 4
Belmont, California

Book Paper
60 lb. Bookbinder's Matte

Printing
Murray Printing Company
Westford, Massachusetts

Nigel Gifford

Welcome to OVER THE HILL But Not Out to Lunch!, a collection of interviews with 49 men and women over age 40 who are physically fit and active, and leading unique and interesting lives.

They are a diverse group, not just in age, but in occupations, sports, approaches to life and attitudes toward diet, training and prevention of injuries. They are not—with a few exceptions—world class athletes. Workouts have to be integrated with busy schedules and other high-priority activities: family, work and travel.

In this book they share their training tips, eating habits, and the secrets to their fitness, enthusiasm and lust for life.

Contents

Contents

Introduction

A few years ago I ran across an old college friend. I hardly recognized him; Sherm had gained a lot of weight since our Stanford days—too many years of a desk job, rich foods and inactivity. Then I lost track of him until my brother sent me a newspaper clipping. Sherm, at age 47, had just run his 100th marathon!

He'd started walking in the evenings after work, instead of "having a drink and a heavy dinner." Then jogging, then running, and finally racing. Along the way he eliminated red meat, fatty foods, hard liquor . . . and about 50 pounds.

I began talking to other high school and college friends, all over 40. Many of them had reassessed their lifestyles and decided that professional and economic success didn't mean that much unless they felt good physically. They had started (or resumed) working out, and found that exercise and a good diet were vital elements for a positive outlook and continued health and well-being.

These personal revelations coincided with the changing times. In the early '60s as a young insurance broker, I decided to start running on my lunch hour. I'd put on a full sweatsuit with an old pair of Keds, pull the sweatshirt hood over my head and run furtively through San Francisco's back alleys so none of my clients would recognize me. At the time, bodybuilding was strictly for weirdos, no one knew what "aerobic" meant, and only super-athletes ran races or marathons.

During the '70s the attitude started to change. Massive amounts of information on the benefits of exercise emerged through magazines, books, TV and word-of-mouth. An amazing variety of new activities and new sports became available to anyone interested in losing weight, building cardiovascular capacity or improving muscle tone.

New equipment, from comfortable running shoes to weight training machines, and a new attitude which encouraged everyone, regardless of present condition, to just get out there and give it a try, made possible the discovery of latent physical talents. With the dawn of the '80s, countless Americans who a decade before would have quietly slipped into "middle age," were now getting back in touch with their bodies for the first time since high school. The spirit was contagious, and the positive effects spilled over into other areas: improved alertness and concentration, more overall energy and reduction of stress.

They'd discovered that muscles are meant to be used, that the heart is healthy when it is made to pump strongly several times a week, that tendons and ligaments need to be stretched, flexed and stressed to maintain their elasticity and function, that the skin has a healthy glow when the body has been moving and the blood circulating.

No wonder corporations began installing gyms and showers, hotels began building fitness facilities for travelers and insurance companies lowered premiums for physically fit clients. Millions of people are now running or working out in parks, along waterfronts and in the streets. Running, pumping iron and sweating is replacing martinis and roast beef for lunch.

With a vague image of OVER THE HILL in mind, I interviewed five old friends: Bill Bullis, Don Manoukian, Pete Thigpen, Sherman Welpton and Dick Zanuck. With three of them I went along on a typical day's workout, then we sat around with a tape recorder afterwards and talked. It was a lot of fun, an excuse to renew old friendships and discuss various meanderings through life over the past 30 years. The revelation that we'd all found working out to be such a vital ingredient in our daily lives seemed timely, worth sharing.

We printed up several hundred copies of these five interviews. These weren't drab or deadly serious how-to accounts by super jocks or born-again movie star fitness gurus, but normal human beings talking freely and openly about fitness as a part of life.

The response was remarkable. People wrote or called. They were inspired and amused; they wanted to take part. Many told us about "this person you've got to interview." We printed a second booklet of six interviews and the feedback and referrals kept coming. One interview led to another and pretty soon a book was under way.

What began as a personal quest to verify elements that I found necessary for my own life and sanity became answers, inspiration and a sense of community: a shared belief that staying fit and physically tuned as the years pass is not only possible, but essential to a whole and positive approach to life. Those of us past the bloom of youth don't have to gain weight, get stiff or stop moving. There's too much to do to start slowing down now.

Doug Ackerman

Doug Ackerman, a Honolulu architect, started getting a stiff neck in the 1960s. Doug is 6'3" and constantly bending over a drafting board put a lot of strain on his back, spine and neck. Also he found that stress–both in his professional and personal life–contributed to an increasingly painful and debilitating condition.

After consulting an orthopedic surgeon, an internist and a chiropractor–with no lasting results–Doug found two books that started him on the road to recovery: one on overcoming stress, another on self treatment and exercises for back pain.

By the time I talked to Doug he'd done enough–on his own–to virtually eliminate the pain of a herniated disc and was once again able to run, windsurf and work at his drafting board.

Doug was a competitive swimmer at Stanford, swimming 100 yards in 22:04 and, having been born in Hawaii, a surfer. He does mostly residential architectural design and many of his houses look remarkably like the old style Hawaiian designs–made of modern materials, but with large roofs, big overhangs, lots of decks, houses suited to local weather and the Hawaiian style.

Vital Statistics

Doug Ackerman, 51
Date of Birth: November 25, 1934
Born: Honolulu, Hawaii
Height: 6'3" **Weight**: 175
Job: Architect
Lives in: Honolulu, Hawaii
Activities: Windsurfing, surfing, running

We had a recession there for awhile and there was no work. Everybody in town was suffering. So when I finally did get some work I was really pushing myself. A lot of stress. Also, I'm tall so everywhere I'd go I'd have to scrunch down. Instead of bending my legs, I'd bend my neck. I'd get in these real awkward positions and just sit there a long time. Gradually my neck was going out but I didn't realize it because it was referred pain down my back.

What was the effect on you?

I would get totally ticked off at everything. I'd be driving along behind a slow truck and try to force it to go faster. For awhile there I'd wake up in the middle of the night with my heart fluttering real fast. I thought I was dying or having a heart attack. I got to the point where I was anxious and depressed about everything, my stomach was bothering me, little things upset me. I started reading books on stress and I finally found *The Quieting Reflex.* The author had been through all the disciplines: Transcendental Meditation, Zen Buddhism . . . He found that doing meditation half an hour a day lowered your tension while you did it, but for the rest of the day you'd build it up again. So he concluded that with every little upset that comes along, you tell yourself, "Wait a minute. I'm going to relax. I'm not going to plug into this upset. I'm just going to let it go." If you do that all day long, he said, within a few weeks or months, you get into the habit.

There must be more to it.

That's all there is to it. It's incredible.

So now if you're out today and get behind that truck, what do you do?

I say, "Wait a minute. Just relax." I'm conscious of being upset before it builds up. It's so simple and yet it's so much more effective than other stress-reducing techniques. It works. I got rid of all my tension about a year and a half ago, but I still had neck and back problems. I'd been to the orthopedist, I'd been to the internist, I'd been to the chiropractor. In essence, they told me, "Well, you're getting older. These things happen." And somehow I couldn't buy that. One day I ran across another book, *Free Yourself from Back Pain.* What a revelation! First of all he says that most of the ailments of the elderly are from misuse of your system instead of aging. The other thing is that the body is tremendously recuperative if you know how to give it a chance. He also said there are a bunch of muscles along the spine that interconnect the vertebrae and those muscles and the ligaments and the bones all form a team in there to hold you upright. And if you let your muscles weaken, you get pain in your ligaments. Lots of older people start slouching because their muscles are not strong enough to hold them upright. What happens is you hang on your ligaments, put a lot of extra pressure on your disc and ligaments and the connective tissue, and the bone starts sending out calcium into the connective tissue. You start getting spurs coming out your

Most of the ailments of the elderly are from the misuse of your system instead of aging.

vertebrae. If you let the thing go, the whole spine starts to become calcified. Everything starts fusing together.

So you started doing these exercises?

Yes, and gradually I've gotten rid of most of my pain.

What do you do now?

I do exercises from the book about 1-1½ hours a day.

What's the result? Can you run?

Oh, yeah. I feel twice as strong when I'm running. I have twice the energy. I do a lot of windsurfing, and I go skiing. I don't need as much sleep. I get excited again where I used to be contantly depressed from the stress and pain. Everything has come back.

□

Sally Cole

Doug with his windsurfer on the North Shore of Oahu, Hawaii

Bob Anderson

When Bob Anderson was 23 and a P. E. major at Cal State Long Beach in southern California, he was overweight, had an ulcer and felt bad most of the time. One day he went for a jog with a friend and couldn't go a mile without stopping. "Here I was going to be a P.E. teacher and tell kids how to get in shape and I was this big slug. I felt like my life needed to change."

Bob started running a mile a day and stopped eating sugar. In spite of the pain and discomfort at first he stuck with it. Soon he was down from 190 lbs. to 155. In the process he found he couldn't get close to touching his toes, so he started stretching... and stretching... and stretching.

What started as an individual pursuit grew to a group activity as Bob's running friends joined him. As time passed, Bob became increasingly flexible and correspondingly excited about how this made his running and other activities more enjoyable. Soon he was teaching his technique to others–to college football teams and then to the L.A. Dodgers. He then wrote, and his wife Jean illustrated, the book Stretching *in 1975. In four years they sold over 35,000 copies out of their basement.*

I got their home-made book in the late '70s, started doing the stretches and eventually asked Bob and Jean if they'd like to revise the book and get it into bookstores. They agreed and we rented them a beach house in Bolinas for four months while we all worked on the new version of the book. In 1980 it was published and to this date it's sold over 500,000 copies.

Vital Statistics

Bob Anderson, 40
Date of Birth: March 20, 1945
Born: Fullerton, California
Height: 5'8½" **Weight**: 145
Job: Author & consultant
Lives in: Palmer Lake, Colorado
Activities: Running, cycling, weight training, stretching

Pretty soon after I started running I lost 30 pounds. Then I decided I'd ride my bike to college every day, so I was running and cycling. I just fell in love with working out. The stretching seemed perfect for running because it was helping my endurance. I found I wasn't so stiff, I could last longer before I got tired. So I got real limber. I could do the splits, the pancake. Before that I couldn't even touch my toes. At school I became an example of self improvement. One of the teachers used to have me in and show his class a picture of me at 190 and say, "Here he is before. Here he is after." *(Laughter)*

What do you do now to work out?

In summer I try to run and cycle three hours in combination. Several times a week I'll be out there 4-5 hours a day. A couple times a week I'll do three workouts a day, the rest of the week it's twice a day. Run in the morning, cycle in the afternoon.

What do you tell people when they ask you about getting started?

I tell them that exercise renews you. But the best things about it you can't put into words. Like running brings back my memories of childhood... the smell of leaves, grass, the early morning mist, good times. It releases things I've forgotten about. And there are all these little explosions taking place inside your body that dissipate stress.

How about when they say they've started but can't keep it up?

The problem is always sticking with it. At first you're excited, but then you lose enthusiasm and quit. The most important thing is to have a good time. I tell them to get some variety, don't just do the same thing day after day. Be creative, entertain yourself. Maybe run one day, cycle another, swim another. Or if running is the main thing, change your route, your pace or the time of day. Turn right instead of left. Stop and enjoy the view and while you're doing that, stretch. You can also change workouts with the season. Don't force yourself to run in the winter if it's icy. Do weight training or aerobic dance or cross-country skiing.

Another thing people shouldn't do is set outlandish goals. Like your "type A" personality will expect quick results. You've got to realize your limitations. Some people who haven't exercised in years will think they're in better shape than they are. Like my friend Hazel, who's 58, says, "I feel 35, but when I look in the mirror I realize I'm 58."

Do you think many people quit because they burn out?

People are torturing themselves less than they did 4 or 5 years ago. They're more into getting to know themselves and finding the activities they really like. There are also so many more

Most people who work at desks get creeping rigor mortis.

Lloyd Kahn, Jr.

Bob and Jean Anderson

activities to choose from, people do things they like, not just what happens to be popular at the moment.

Running is a good example. So many people got into it, got some early benefits and then got carried away. They'd run 60 miles a week, or just pound out that mileage every day. Now they're getting smarter. Counting your pulse beats or keeping a log is important–you know, the scientific approach. But what's more important to me is the enjoyment of it, how it makes me feel. Most of the time I forget about all the mileage, numbers, pulse and speed.

When I was in college it was a revelation to find out I could enjoy exercise. "You mean you actually like this stuff?" Instead of, "Uh, it's killing me, I'm going to feel so good when it's done." I found out that my *body* wanted to go for a workout. It wanted to have the blood circulate faster, to bring in more oxygen. Muscles and ligaments want to be worked. The only problem, often, is the mind. The other day a guy was telling me he had no time to run. I said "Look, get up an hour earlier than usual. No matter how cold it is or how much you don't want to, get up and take a short run. Then when you come back, after you shower and go to work, ask yourself if it was worth it. You know the answer to that. He'll feel better all day long. His mind will be clearer. You know, you never hear anyone say, "God, I'm so sorry I worked out."

What do you think about life after 40?

When we were little kids, we never sat still. Then we went to school and started sitting. In high school we got a car. In college there's more sitting, or you get into a specific sport. Typically when you get out of college you get a job, have kids, get less physical activity and sit at a desk the rest of your life. Maybe around age 26, you start putting on weight. Three or four pounds a year is 30-40 pounds in 10 years. Life after 40 can be real good, or it can be awful.

Most people who work at desks get creeping rigor mortis. They are losing their contact with the physical world. As we get older, we find ourselves in rigid positions, sitting or standing. We lose joint flexibility and muscle elasticity. Look around at your friends, at all the problems they're having by not being able to move like they could when they were young. It's not really how old you are that's important, it's how you feel. □

Jean Anderson

Bob runs 2-3 hours daily in the hills behind his home near Colorado Springs, Colorado.

Everyday Stretches

Here are 12 basic everyday stretches by Bob and Jean Anderson that will help keep you flexible and limber.

General stretching rules:

- Stretch slowly and with control.
- Don't compare your flexibility with others.
- The key is to *relax*.
- Breathing should be slow, deep, rhythmical.
- Don't hold breath while stretching.
- Don't bounce.
- No pain.
- Hold only stretch tensions that feel good.

Shaded areas indicate body parts being stretched.

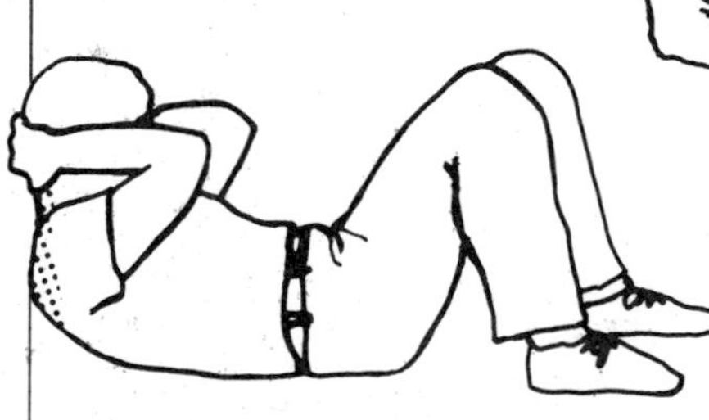

1. Start with head on floor. *Slowly* raise until you feel a slight stretch. Hold 5 seconds. Repeat 3 times.

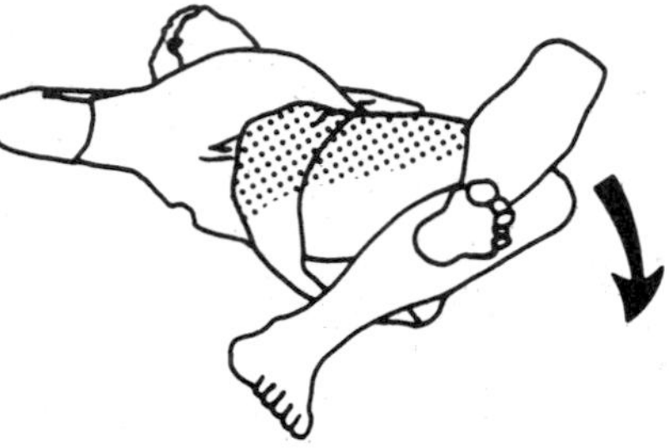

2. Fingers interlaced behind head. Slowly pull right leg down with left. Hold 30 seconds. Repeat for other side.

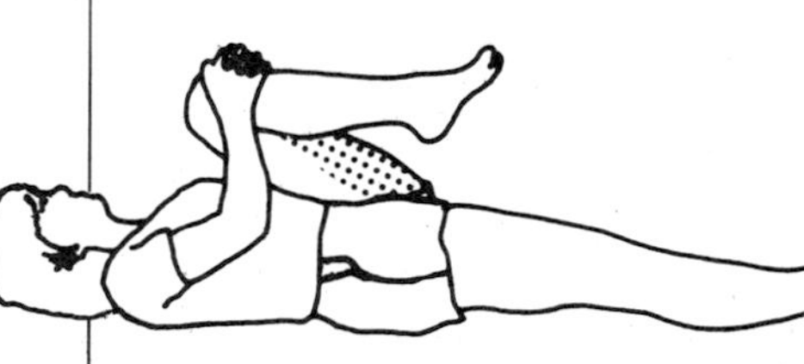

3. Next straighten both legs & relax. Then pull each leg toward chest. Hold 30 seconds.

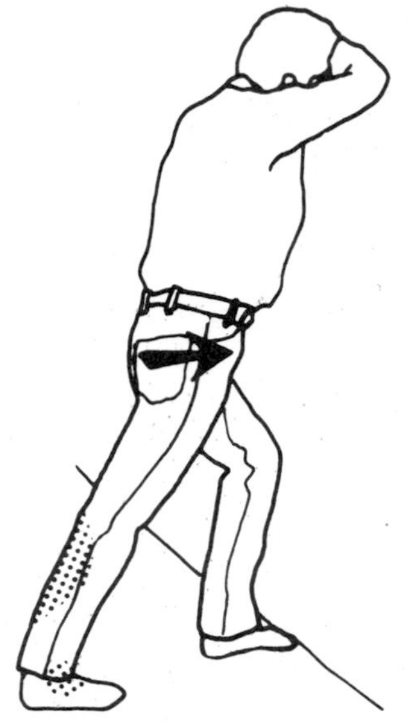

4. Lean against wall. *Toes pointed straight ahead.* Keep heel of straight leg on ground. Slowly move hips forward. Hold 30 seconds. Do both legs.

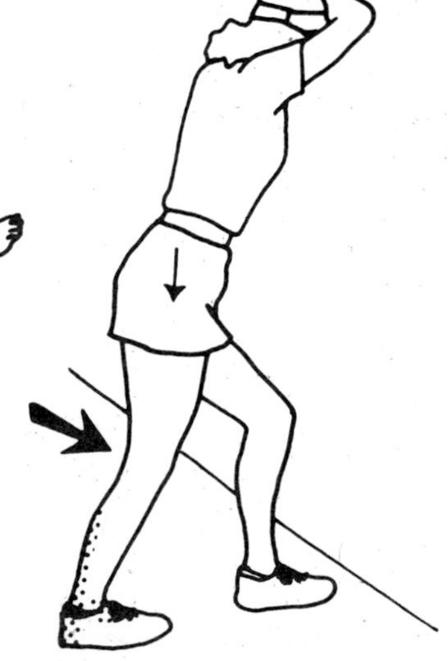

5. Slightly bend back knee, keeping foot flat. 15 seconds each leg. Go until you feel only a *slight stretch* here.

6. Interlace fingers, palms upward. Push arms slightly back and up. Hold 15 seconds.

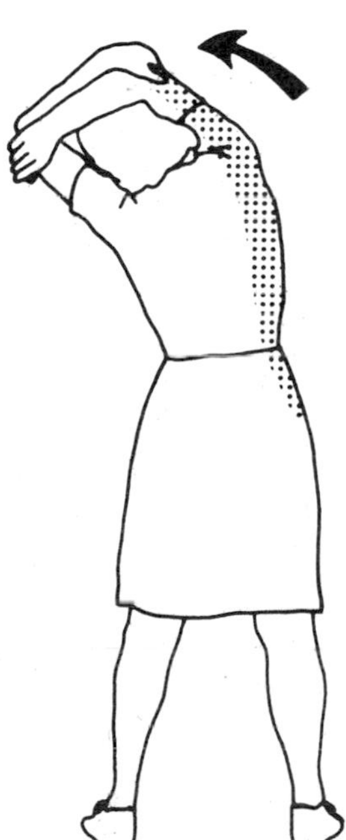

7. Pull elbow behind head as you bend hips slightly to side. 10 seconds each side.

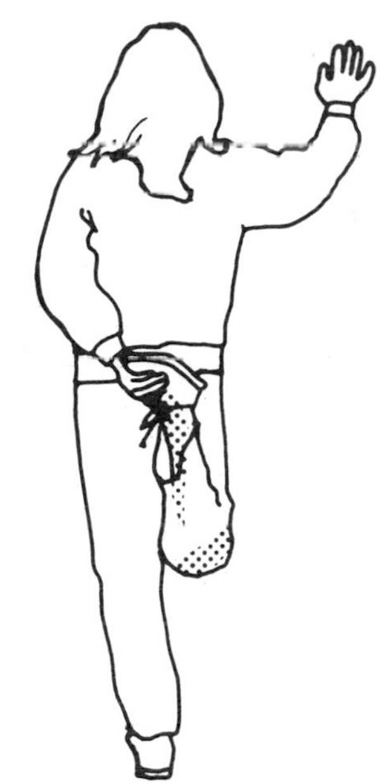

8. Right hand to left foot and stretch gently. Hold 30 seconds. Do other side. Good for problem knees and knee rehab.

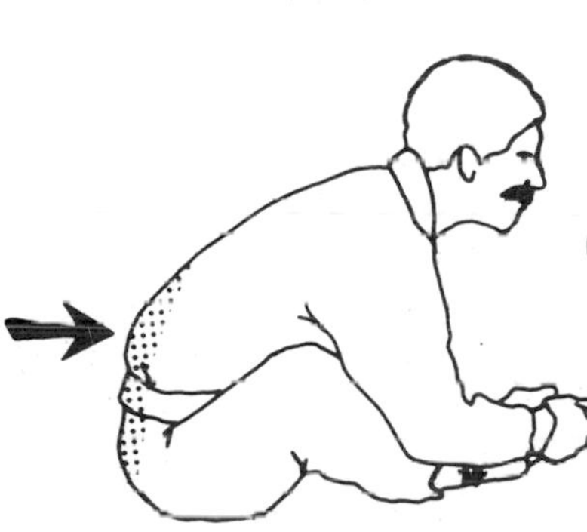

9. Soles of feet together. Pull forward gently bending from hips, not shoulders. Hold 30 seconds.

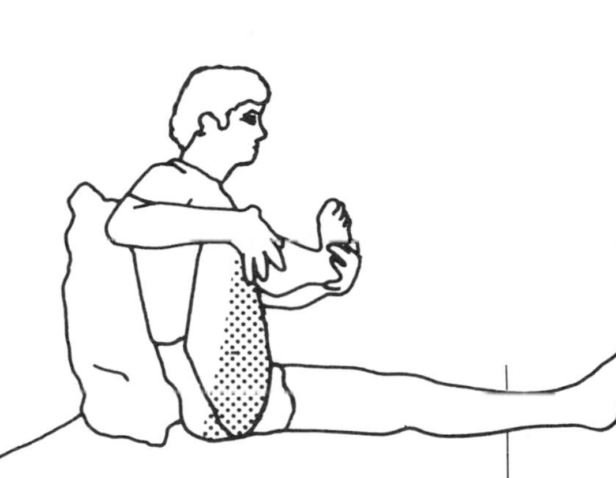

10. Gently pull leg toward chest. Hold 30 seconds. Do other leg. Pull leg as one unit so there's no stress in knee.

11. Slowly turn head to look over left shoulder as you rotate upper body to left. Right arm keeps left leg stationary. Hold 15 seconds, do other side.

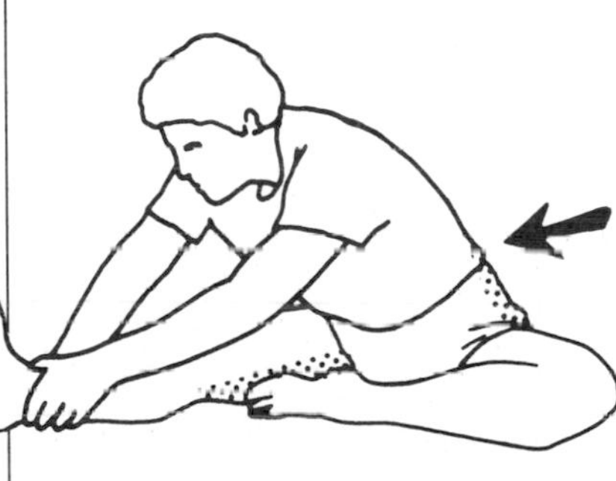

12. Slowly bend forward from hips until you feel slight stretch. Hold 15 seconds. After muscles have relaxed lean forward a bit more. Hold another 15 seconds. Do other side. □

Janet Baer

I'd last seen Janet Baer in 1982. At the time we had a dairy goat and Janet and her husband Lew had a small herd on their 3-acre farm near Sebastopol, California. Janet was a poet, a painter, a gourmet cook and an articulate enthusiast for life in general. Lew edited a monthly newsletter for Northern California goat owners called Goat Notes. *He was a good writer and editor and I'd been talking to him about doing a book on dairy goats. But as time passed, I gave up on the goats (too much work!) and lost touch with the Baers.*

One day I called them up and when Janet asked what I was doing, I mentioned Over the Hill.

"Well, I'm just over 40," said Janet, "and you know, I've lost 130 pounds."

Huh? I'd known people to lose 15 or 20 pounds, but 130 . . . ? The voice on the phone was the same, but the body attached to it was now less than half its former volume. I asked Janet a few questions, and began thinking, what a great example for people who want to lose weight. She just decided to take action, did it and the result was sensational, inspirational. Right?

Well, not exactly . . . As the story unfolded, it turned out things were not as truly fabulous as they sounded at first. Janet was delighted with how she looked and felt, but what she was having to do to maintain her new weight—with respect to diet and exercise—was formidable.

Apparently when you lose a lot of weight, your body in its wisdom and instinct for survival becomes highly efficient in its utilization of energy. It's as if, shocked by sudden weight loss, the body doesn't burn, but rather stores away the food—as fat. (This is the way the body stores energy.) After over a year Janet's metabolism hadn't kicked into normal (she says it's the same for everyone else she knows who's lost weight this way). Even with a tremendous amount of exercising, it's impossible to eat anywhere near a normal amount of food. The body just doesn't burn it up.

Janet was candid and forthright about her situation. There were some great things about what she'd done, but there was also the question: was it worth it? The reality turned out quite a bit different from the vision.

> *Between the idea*
> *And the reality*
> *Between the motion*
> *And the act*
> *Falls the Shadow.*
> *– T.S. Eliot*

I talked to Janet in February, then again six months later. The last time, it seemed as if she'd begun to balance the pendulum swing from one extreme to another, and was finding some middle ground.

I feel better now because I'm super-charged, but I also felt good before. Now I'm real, real dynamic. I'm sleek and elegant. For a poet, you look wonderful on stage. But then I looked good on stage when I was big too because I have great exuberance and love of myself, and it doesn't matter if that's a fat self or a thin self. *(Laughter)* So that kind of celebration of the self, I've always had that. Some fat people don't. Some fat people sit home and feel miserable, "I'm fat, I'm fat." I'm such a creature of the spirit that it's the ideas and the spirit and the things I create that are what I am.

If you were going to start over again, knowing what you know now . . .

Knowing what I know now, I wouldn't have done it. I would have stayed just as I was. I'm very happy with the way I look and feel now, but it is not a satisfactory lifestyle for a creative, indulgent, passionate person. The fast didn't bother me because I'm very Zen and abstinence is lovely. Abstinence is not denial. It's a time of putting away, of mellowing out. Though I must admit I missed eating. All the time I would have these flashes, I would smell tamales out of nowhere. But then when you start to eat and you have to control it strictly, that's horrid. That is denial. It's sadistic.

How long was the fast?

Well, mine was 9½ months.

***9½ months?* What kind of fast?**

It's called a protein sparing modified fast. I ate nothing. I took a protein supplement so that I wouldn't have heart or kidney damage and a potassium supplement so my muscles would continue to function. And that's it.

Vital Statistics

Janet Baer, 43
Date of Birth: August 5, 1942
Born: San Francisco, California
Height: 5'4" **Weight**: See interview
Job: Poet, painter, cook
Lives in: Penngrove, California
Activities: Tai Chi, aerobic dance, exercycle

The more you starve that body into losing that weight the more that body wants to regain it afterwards.

Had you considered a less radical approach?

If you're really overweight, a less radical approach isn't gonna do it. It doesn't matter how the weight gets lost, this lost it faster. If I did something like Weight Watchers, it would take me 3 years to do what I did in a year.

Did you consult with doctors or a clinic?

I had observed what different people had done, and they were all unsuccessful. This program attracted me because they said that if you put out more calories in exercise than food coming in, you will lose. Now that makes sense. So I learned how to exercise a tremendous amount so I could eat well. And now I'm in a trap. Here I am in a very strong, lovely body, completely unable to eat anything because my metabolism is so low. I'm holding my weight well but at tremendous psychological cost. Tremendous.

The psychological cost is in putting all that time into working out or in not being able to eat?

Both. I want to eat so very, very much I'm willing to put up with the terrible inroads into my time so that I can eat well. But I've found I get nothing back. The program tells you your skin will get dry, you will have some hair loss, you will lose your sexual drive, and you'll be grouchy while you're fasting. They make you sign a thing saying you won't sue them if you go insane because of the process. But they don't tell you that about half the people become so

Lloyd Kahn, Jr.

Lloyd Kahn, Jr.

slowed in their metabolism that they can essentially never eat again.

What was the first thing you ate when you came off your fast?

Everybody asked me that. The first thing I ate was a piece of French bread. When you come off you can't eat a complete meal for quite awhile.

You mean you hadn't eaten any bread or vegetables for 9 months?

Absolutely nothing. I remember I was at a party and I passed this wonderful plate of fudge cake down to the lady next to me and I got a big glob of chocolate icing on my thumb. I wiped it off on my napkin. I mean I did not lick my finger. I developed that kind of control. I can impose that on my eating habits the rest of my life and stay very thin and very lovely but not enjoy anything either. It's not like I'm trapped being fat; I'm trapped being thin. That's why you hear me speaking with two voices.

What's your attitude toward food?

Well, I think food should be really good. I think it's absolutely sinful to eat anything and not enjoy it, whatever that may be. Whether it's skim milk, yogurt, eat the best kind you can find. If it's chocolate eclairs, don't eat frozen ones, make them yourself and make them good. You know, I really believe in excellence in all things. That's why I'm successful in having lost the weight. I'm a great hedonist and I only live to enjoy. You can't accomplish anything unless you're honest with yourself. I know where I'm at.

You're quite a cook, aren't you?

Yeah. So I'm deprived of one of my 3 greatest creative ventures.

Poetry, cooking and . . . ?

Painting . . . You know I like to participate richly in what I do . . . so I'm not satisfied with half a cup of skim milk yogurt and one cracker. I want egg rolls. *(Laughter)* And I can make 15 kinds.

Were you heavy as a kid?

Yes, but I didn't look heavy. I matured about 3 years earlier than the other girls. So I just looked rather womanly. I didn't look big, just different. I wasn't fat, but I was never lean either. And I've noticed now that girls that go into puberty 10 lbs. heavy, in five years are 40 lbs. heavy.

Did you just put on a few pounds a year for 20 years?

Yeah, but I had a big headstart because at age 11 I weighed like 130 when people my size were just cracking 100.

What did you get up to last year when you started to take it off?

242. And I'm only 5'4" tall.

How much do you weigh now?

I was 125 this morning.

What do you eat in a day now?

If I want to keep the weight, 1000 calories a day. Yesterday, I had 2 ounces of chicken, 4 cups of air popped popcorn, skim milk, yogurt, lettuce and dressing (Japanese dressing made with saccharine instead of sugar) and that was it.

Do you ever eat out?

Sometimes. But that may be the only time I eat all week. I weigh all the calories and food I eat. So now I can estimate most things very well. The first time we go to a particular restaurant, I usually bring my scale and little measures. The first time we went for Dim Sum, I weighed all my things. I took the filling out and weighed the filling. But I don't like that kind of frugality. I want to enjoy. I want to be part of the world, to participate . . . I gotta be me. I'm not myself when I'm abstaining.

Maybe it's just a matter of time until the metabolism gets working.

All the things you read about how to raise your metabolism, I've done them and more. They say exercise more. You cannot exercise more than 8 or 9 hours a day. And I don't like having to schedule my time. I like to *wake* when I am done sleeping. I like to *write* as I need to. I like to move with the wind, so I really resent having to live a structured life. It's like I'm in a box.

What's a typical day's workout for you?

Monday, Wednesday and Friday, I get up at 6:15 and I beg another 15 minutes out of Lew and the alarm clock. Usually I sleep in my leotard so that I spring out of bed, go to the bathroom and weigh myself. I make a pot of tea and I drink a half a cup of bran with raisins in it, maybe. If I'm looking forward to a nice meal later that day, I will not have the raisins. Then I get on the bike and ride from 7 till 9:20. Then I fly out of here to my aerobics class. And I do two classes back to back. That takes me up until noon. I usually spend 10 minutes B.S.'ing after class and I do my weights till 1 o'clock. Then I either go home and ride the exercise bike or work 3 hours on my poetry. I get back on the bike about 4 o'clock, sometimes 5, and intermittently I will ride until midnight. On Monday I always do because "Hart to Hart" is on and then "Columbo." I have never been able to take television without doing 2 other things anyway.

Have you tried running?

I don't want to run. I mean I don't like the jarring. There's no way I'm going to run out in the cold, dogs chasing me. And you can't talk when you . . . I like to read, to write, to talk and to eat. How can you read, write and talk while you're running? So the bike is just great for me. Here I am, we're having a nice conversation *(Janet was on her exercycle when we did this interview).*

And you're getting some exercise.

Yes, here I am. I'm myself. I can talk. I'm making this elaborate Greek dinner tonight so I'm reading my cookbooks. I've got a poem to revise for a workshop. And I'll be on the bike except when I'm cooking, except when we're at the poetry thing, except when our company's here. And they'll probably leave about midnight and I will ride a couple of hours before I go to bed. I don't need much sleep now . . . about 4 hours.

I've got that kind of body now. I don't like competitive sports. Well, you know, I don't like moving at all. But when I move I like to move very beautifully. If I weren't a poet, an artist and a chef, I would get into my Tai Chi.

What would you tell somebody who wants to lose a lot of weight?

It is possible to lose it, but it's long and boring. Keeping it off is the trick. It means a radical change in lifestyle. It's wonderful to be thin, it really is. It's a great delight, especially for a woman. I mean it's really jazzy. I love it. I do love pleasure more and I want both. I want it all. The reason I did this whole thing . . . Lew said, "Why don't you just lose 50 lbs. and be done with it?" If I'd lost 50 lbs., I still would have been a fat woman. You would gain it right back because you wouldn't have the incentive to keep it off. So now I have tremendous incentive to keep it off because I look so beautiful.

Have you thought of getting a few opinions about what is happening with your metabolism?

With any weight loss, you have this problem. But most people lose at the most 15 or 20 pounds. So it's not that evident. But here I've lost 130 so you can imagine how the body has had to slow itself in order to survive. The more you starve that body into losing that weight the more that body wants to regain it afterwards.

The set point theory. *(A theory that the body has a complex mechanism in the brain that attempts to maintain the current level of body fat.)*

If they told you the truth . . . they'd say, "Well, some of the people are just not going to be able to eat no matter what they do." But the program wouldn't make so much money. They say, "Well, most everyone does splendidly." Well, most everyone drops out of the project. Now some people's metabolism kicks into normal in a few weeks. Some people's never does. A large body takes a lot more food to run it, but this large body never moved at all. At all! And now this little body runs like a gazelle, and really doesn't need to eat. I know a lot of people who are into athletics now and almost all of them can eat like horses because they work hard. I had a perfectly normal metabolism before I began this.

I still think you're going to end up weighing some more and you're going to be able to cut your exercising in half.

Well, I won't speculate. Everyone said, "Oh, you're never going to get fat again." That makes me angry because I don't know what I'm going to do. I'm not locked into anything. You know, if it becomes intolerable, you must change it before you go nuts, before you lose your feelings for life.

Six months later I talked to Janet again. She had by now moderated her extreme diet/exercise program. She had gained 20-25 lbs. and wasn't sure if her weight would stabilize.

How much are you exercycling now?

About 50 miles a day, an hour and a half.

And what aerobics classes?

I do 3 aerobics classes a week. And I lift some weights.

Sounds more human.

Well, that's all I'm willing to do. I went all the way. I wanted to eat well. I wanted the whole thing to work. I never want to go through that kind of deprivation again. When I was working out all day, there was no quiet time for contemplation, for other good things. I tried to do both, but I could see that the chemical change in the brain is radical. It's not into doing anything except working that body. There is a change in the body and for hours after that kind of exercise, there is no slack time for creative thought. The body is too charged up; the brain is boosted so high it doesn't calm down. And for the creative things, that brain has to be calm. The heart has to be agitated but the brain has to be calm. And here it was the other way around. The brain was so agitated and the heart calm . . . You get this incredibly productive body but that doesn't write poems, that doesn't paint pictures, that doesn't keep your love alive . . . . □

HEAVY LAMENT

Sipping bitter tea, I set my rice-filled bowl
before the shrine.
What I endure, I bear alone, but not in solitude:
this endless stream of aching empty hours.

I will be serene,
a Buddha, turning inward, not away --
the eightfold path embraces,
like the octopus, with arms that taper down
to nothingness, feeling in the dark
the way cool waters flow . . .
From freedom's fire, I leap a lotus ring,
wondering still if there are dreams beyond desire.
Within the round perfection of their shells --
come silent snails -- to soothe away these sorrows:
As each ounce burns, hungers rise
to growl like tigers prowling in the brain.

Choosing the middle way, there are no sacraments;
I know the water-torture from within.
To become as water, seeping up among the mosses,
following the rocks' etched watercourse,
each day more deep,
surely I am edging toward the cliff --
the breathless fall cascading down the fractures of the face;
the water splits to foam,
and air accepts the vapor as its own.

Streams of many seasons pass;
the scent of flowers travels with the wind.
Seeking enlightenment no more,
I wait for quince buds opening.
Ink strokes smooth against the stone;
I watch the shades diffuse and dip my brush.
Words run wet with simple elegance;
there is only now and this white paper --
a warm splash . . . of satori . . . rushing over.

–Janet Baer

Marsha Bancroft

Jim Reme

Marsha Bancroft is a marathon runner and triathlete. She has a best marathon time of 3:18 and has competed in triathlons of the "Tin Man" variety: 1.2 mile swim, 25 mile bike ride and 10 mile run. She works out six days a week, running, swimming, cycling and weight training, yet she hasn't given up her profession, deserted her family or alienated her friends. She's an executive of the largest press clipping service in the country, is happily married (to a husband who fully supports her athletic activities), has raised twin daughters, age 22, and a son, age 19, and seems to be having a lot of fun with a busy, productive and healthy life.

When you were in college what did you think you were going to do?

Get married and have children. I never had any encouragement to have a career.

That would have been in the '60s.

Yeah. I didn't think about fitness or diet or anything like that in those years. I was physically active. I was a professional horsewoman for 12 years and that kept me on my feet all day. And I played lots of racquetball. But I did that because I was interested in it, not specifically for fitness.

In those years there wasn't the consciousness of how good working out made you feel. I started running and focusing on fitness when I gained some weight. The more you run, the more involved with fitness you get because you want to do whatever is going to improve your running.

In the '60s, I became more aware that I could do whatever I wanted to do. I didn't have to fit into anybody's idea of what women should do. Realizing that really helped me.

Talk about your running career.

I started running in '79. After awhile, I tried a local race and won my age group. That really turned me on. It was a two-mile race. I moved up to 5K's and then 10K's. The next year I qualified for the New York Marathon.

That race was fantastic. One of the best, most incredible experiences of my life. Really. It was a goal I'd set for myself and to actually do it... That picture you have of my friends and I crossing the finish line together, Avon used that in all its 1982 advertisements. Amazing.

After New York, I decided to try to qualify for Boston. I did and that race was a remarkable experience too. The people there just pick you up and carry you along. I didn't hit the wall, but I did cramp up and was in a lot of pain. But I finished. I was so happy to finish.

I had a stress fracture after that, so I backed off long distance running. I started biking, running and swimming. I met some triathletes, and decided to become one. I entered a United States Triathlon Association Series race in New York. The course was awful. It was longer than it was supposed to be, and the hilliest, hardest course imaginable. People joked that no California people came to race 'cause the course was too hard. *(Laughter)* They're used to it flat. But I did it, and now I've done 7 triathlons in all.

Are triathletes different from runners?

I think triathletes are more fun and relaxed. But they're still hard-nosed and strong willed about training. People like me, instead of burning out on the fact we can't always win because of our age-level or physical condition, we compete with ourselves-we push ourselves in training.

What's your training like?

I run 6 miles, 6 days a week at 5:30 A.M. Then I go to the Nautilus 3 times a week, I swim during lunch about half a mile, and I bike 2-3 times a week in the evening.

Does all that training cause problems with your family?

It never has. My husband is very supportive. He promotes me in a sense. It's amazing. I don't think everybody has that kind of relationship.

How about food?

Well, I can't eat anything actually. I have very low metabolism. My resting pulse is about 42. I'm an "easy keeper"—that's what we used

> **Vital Statistics**
> Marsha Bancroft, 48
> **Date of Birth**: January 17, 1938
> **Born**: West Palm Beach, Florida
> **Height**: 5'3" **Weight**: 117
> **Job**: Sales manager
> **Lives in**: Essex Fells, New Jersey
> **Activities**: Running, swimming, cycling, Nautilus

I don't eat sugar, I don't eat any salt, and I don't eat any fat. I stay very close to Pritikin.

Jane Sobel—Janeart

Left to right: Marsha Bancroft, Jane Sandelands, Antonia Mills finishing Avon International Marathon together in 1982

to say about horses—you don't have to feed me very much and I'll stay alive.

Even with all that training?

Yes. My system is extremely efficient. I don't eat sugar, I don't eat any salt, and I don't eat any fat. I stay very close to Pritikin. I use a little bit of diet margarine, like maybe a tablespoon a day, but other than that I don't eat any fried foods, no cheese. I eat eggs once a week. And no meat. I eat poultry and fish.

Is it hard to maintain that or are you used to it?

No, the only thing that is hard for me is portion control. I don't crave these other things at all. Because I happen to love carbohydrates. I love pasta and whole grains. I don't like white bread and white rice. I like meat, but I don't miss it at all.

Do you think all this physical activity has any carry-over in your professional work?

Well, your productivity increases, there's no question about it. The interesting thing to me is how doing physical or aerobic exercise at least 3 or 4 times a week contributes to your total well-being and your ability to learn and comprehend and create.□

Paxton Beale

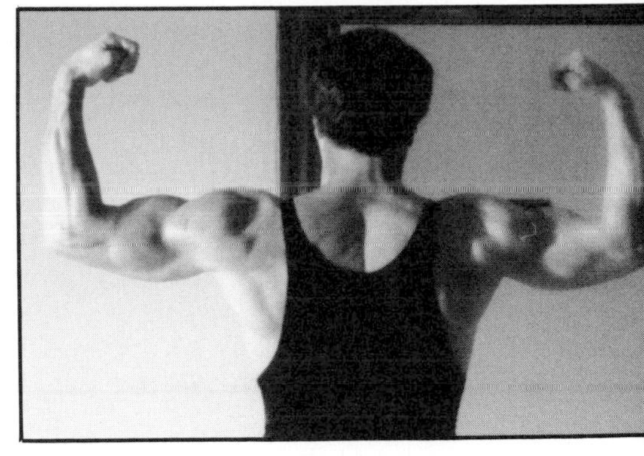

Pax Beale has performed some spectacular athletic stunts over the years. Such as:

- *Running 145 miles in two days through Death Valley and up Mt. Whitney in the hottest month of the year.*
- *Swimming from San Francisco to Alcatraz at night on his 50th birthday in sub-50° water.*
- *Racing a 30,000 ton ocean liner from San Francisco to Alaska on bikes. (Pax and friend Ken Crutchlow won by drafting behind their van.)*
- *Running a 190 mile relay to Reno from S.F. with a friend.*

Pax's latest passion is bodybuilding, which he took up to relieve chronic back pain. When we met at the gym to do this interview it was obvious he'd turned a liability into an asset. When he got warmed up and took off his jacket, it was hard to believe this was the physique of a 56-year-old man. The workout that had developed these muscles consisted of a variety of exercises, each one pushed to the absolute limit. When he got to the point where he couldn't lift the barbell a bit further (and was grunting and howling in pain) he had me come along and with a finger or two gently lift the weight so he could force himself into another realm of agony and muscle exertion.

Based on personal success in treating a severe back problem with exercises, posture and traction, Pax has opened an elaborate back clinic with state-of-the-art equipment in one of his medical facilities in San Francisco.

Vital Statistics
Paxton Beale, 56
Date of Birth: December 12, 1929
Born: Oakland, California
Height: 6'3" **Weight:** 200
Job: Hospital administrator
Lives in: Oakland, California
Activities: Bodybuilding, running, cycling, swimming

What happened to your back?

When I was 13 years old, during World War II, I was working in an Oakland warehouse throwing around furniture. To this day I can remember the type of chair I lifted when my back first went out—it was a platform rocker with concrete in the bottom. I never experienced any pain like that in my life. I thought somebody had driven a spike through the bottom of my back.

In high school, I was the city shotput champion, and also played basketball and football. I should have been good at football but in 3 years I never finished a season because of my back. Then I got an athletic scholarship to the University of California but each year my back would give out on me.

Is your back OK now?

Maybe not perfect but manageable. And that's because I've assumed responsibility for it and I have made a behavioral lifestyle change.

How bad *was* your back?

Well, swimming is supposed to be good for backs. And I couldn't even swim. I stood out there curved like a question mark trying to go in the water. At one point I had a hospital bed next to my desk at the office.

A little anecdote about back pain: Once I broke 2 ankles skiing. Now, my back always hurt when I skied but I'd tolerate it. Back pain is funny. You're good for a week and bad for 3 weeks; good for 2 weeks, bad for one week. It teases you, it tantalizes you. When I broke my ankles and was sitting in the chalet, people would buy me free drinks. Pretty girls would sign my cast. When you have a bum back they look at you like you're a coward, a malingerer. Then I got to where I started dropping out of marathons; I wasn't tired but I was taking shorter and shorter steps. An EMG showed that I'd lost 75% of my response in my right leg. Goddamnit, you run along on the flat and you think you're going uphill. It wasn't a sharp pain. It was a dullness. I'd run along and feel OK, then I'd just be going slower and slower until I was walking. Couldn't get my legs out in front of me. I finally gave up running. It was psychologically depressing. The post-race parties weren't fun any longer. I didn't have anything to talk about. "Hey, how'd you do today?" "Oh, I dropped out." I got to the point where I couldn't identify with the people.

What did you do to improve things?

There is no one area of medicine that has so many different professions trying to tackle the problem. You've got neurosurgeons, orthopedists, podiatrists, chiropractors, acupressurists, acupuncturists, Rolfers, God knows who else . . . And none of them have solved the problem. I used orthotic devices, I had acupressure,

So before I knew it I was on a stage posing in the only over-50 bodybuilding contest in the United States.

acupuncture. I finally had a chymopapain injection up in Canada, which did not work out.

What's that?

They inject a papaya enzyme into your lower spine. It's kind of a chemical that destroys the disc. I had that at 4 locations in my back, but my back was just too shot for it to work.

Discs wrecked?

Oh, yeah. Ruptured, as well as herniated. And I also had some spinal fluid drained out of my spine and had cortisone, which is anti-inflammatory, inserted directly into my spinal column.

Part of the same treatment?

No, that was another time. Totally unrelated to the chymopapain. I also had epidural blocks where they shoot cortisone into the areas of the nerves in the bottom of the spine. Interestingly enough, although I'm a product of organized medicine (medical doctors, that is), I have to admit that the one single profession that relieved my pain to the greatest extent were chiropractors. Except it was temporary. As soon as I went back to working out I just ran into the same problem.

I'd been to several orthopedic surgeons but this one in particular that I had a great deal of respect for scheduled me, with the date given for additional surgery, to have my spine fused at 4 locations and have a triple laminectomy. I mean, it wasn't something I was thinking about doing one of these days, I was *scheduled!* I was scared witless and consulted my navel and said, "There's just *gotta* be some other way."

Looking back, I think my first example of weightlifting was when I had to go to the bathroom at night and couldn't get out of bed. For months I'd have to be helped out of bed, on and off for 2 years. I'd sit down on the toilet with the pain shooting through me. Then I reached over for the roll of toilet paper. *Augh!* Like somebody diggin' a friggin' spike right through my goddamn spine. So I tried my first weightlifting by lifting a roll of toilet paper.

What did you do?

Out of sheer fear and fright I tried to analyze every remedy of these different specialists and I said to myself, "They all have their individual approaches and they're very biased about them, but there are two themes they all have: good posture and traction. These were the common threads. So I said, "Why don't I try to focus on better posture?" With fusion, they're putting metal in your spine and fusing you permanently into what they think is good posture. When you get a medical corset, the purpose of that is to force you into good posture. The chiropractor and the Rolfer are trying to realign your body, hoping to hell you don't slip out of it again. The other alternative was to use your own muscles to self-brace yourself in good posture.

So I said, "I'm going to go to the guys who really know exercise—the weightlifters. I didn't really feel like the medical profession could help me anymore. I don't want to be critical of the surgeons because I work with surgeons, but if you go to school for 16 years to learn how to cut somebody, why do you want to be teaching somebody bent-knee sit-ups? So I said, "It's my job to go out and learn how to do it myself."

I analyzed every muscle group and ruled out the ones I shouldn't work on. No compression-type exercises, like standing calf or deltoid. But I *could* do bench presses. The only trouble was I couldn't get the weights over to the bench. Ask some of the guys who were in the gym, I mean I was a cripple. But out of sheer fear I persevered. Trial and error. I had regressions. But I worked out a regime that was fun and challenging, not boring. I liked the buzz word "behavioral lifestyle change," and I was committed.

I started getting pretty strong but I still couldn't hold good posture. Now most people who want to improve posture need to hold the pelvic tilt. I went down to the YMCA and saw all these people lying on the basketball floor at noontime, practicing the pelvic tilt. That's perfect if you're going to walk around the rest of your life with a basketball court on your back. My problem was how to hold that pelvic tilt while I moved, not just in a static position. I had to learn how to contract my muscles, like bodybuilders do when they go through their posing routines. The mind has to communicate with those muscles to make them fire, i.e., contract. It's not an involuntary occurrence, like blinking your eye. It's a learned experience. So I kept working on those contractions. Then I started learning how to contract my bicep and tricep just to break the monotony of contracting the other ones, you see? And I said, "Well, if

you keep doing this, you hamburger, maybe one of these days you're going to enter a bodybuilding contest." *(Laughter)* So I did. I first approached it with great apprehension. I don't think there's any sport that started so poorly in the public's eye. Everyone thought bodybuilders were kinky, narcissistic, stupid muscle heads. In truth, I went to my first contest because I had learned how to flex my muscles to a degree. I also went and sought out an excellent bodybuilder. This guy knew how to take what medicine had deemed logical to do and with his street smarts make a neophyte like myself be able to do it. Unlike joggers, the old hardcore guys, generally speaking, were not particularly educated people. But there were a ton of Damon Runyon characters in there and I loved 'em. So before I knew it I was on a stage posing in the only over-50 bodybuilding contest in the United States I could find.

Are you going to stick with it?

Absolutely. It's the greatest sport I've ever been involved in in my life. I found the typical bodybuilders (except for those who take steroids) are relatively drug free. They eat good diets, they don't smoke. They get a lot of sleep. They live an amazingly healthy life. I began to think that some of these things these guys were doing, they didn't know why they were working, but they were.

On another subject, tell me about that swim on your 50th birthday.

I wanted to be the first person ever to swim to Alcatraz in the pitch dark. So at 7:18 on my 50th birthday I jumped in and swam to Alcatraz.

How long did it take you?

61 minutes.

7:18 in the evening?

Yeah. In December. That's cold, baby. The Coast Guard was very courteous and agreed to slow down the shipping out there then. What also made it nice was that my lady friend rented the Blue and Gold Fleet boat and invited 350 of my friends, my relatives, my college roommates. And five guys I went to grammar school with. By the time they got in the boat and got out there I was 85% of the way across. Then I heard the Cal fight song ringing out in the middle of the bay on a tape deck. I couldn't believe it! □

Jack Bettencourt

Jack Bettencourt is an all-around athlete. He was a 156 lb. Golden Gloves boxing champion in San Francisco in 1950, boxed for two years at Cal Poly college in California, and lost to Spider Webb (who then lost to Floyd Patterson) in the 1952 Olympic trials. He was training for the 1956 Olympic games in Melbourne when he got married and his wife convinced him to give up boxing.

These days Jack runs, swims, rows and cycles. He competes in triathlons and has done the Ironman twice. His latest times were 1:20 for the 2.4 mile swim, 7:45 for the 118 mile bike ride (even after changing a flat) and 4:55 for the 26.2 mile run. Total time 14 hours. Pretty spectacular for 57 years old!

Is the Ironman swim-start just chaos?

(Laughter) Look at this picture. *(He shows me an aerial photo of 1100 red-hatted swimmers, waiting to start the Ironman.)* That's what it's like. They tell you to seed yourself. If you're fast, get up front. If you're a medium swimmer, in the middle. If you're slow, get in the back. What turmoil!

> **Vital Statistics**
> Jack Bettencourt, 57
> **Date of Birth**: October 23, 1928
> **Born**: San Mateo, California
> **Height**: 5'9" **Weight**: 160
> **Job**: Banker
> **Lives in**: South San Francisco, California
> **Activities**: Running, swimming, cycling, rowing

So the top guys get right up front and sprint to get out of the way.

I would too if I was that fast. I passed a lot of people in the water and I did all right but it takes up time when you start going around people and swimmin' on top of people.

How do you train for the Ironman?

All year long I run and swim and cycle. All I do with three months to go is step it up. I never quit! Three or four months ahead of time I'll start swimming 4-5 miles a week. And I'll start cycling about 200 miles a week and do two 20-mile runs a week. I never quit because I assume I can always do a small triathlon somewhere.

So about 5 or 6 days a week you're training.

Oh, yeah, when I start crankin' up. Otherwise, I'm swimming a mile a day and I'm cycling on weekends. And running a little bit.

Did you grow up in San Francisco?

No, my dad died in 1937. I was 9 years old. I was shipped to my grandfather's ranch in San Mateo County. End of the Depression. My grandfather said he'd raise my brother and I if we worked for our keep. And from the age of 9 or 10 years old we did manual labor in the field, 12-14 hours a day. Mainly cattle and grain.

Did you go to school?

Yeah. We had to get up at 4:30-5:00 and milk cows for an hour. Then go in the house, change our clothes and get ready and run or walk a mile out to the road to catch the bus that took us 14 miles to school. Then go to school, catch the bus, ride 14 miles home, get off the bus, walk a mile down the road, get our clothes changed, go out to the cows, get them in and start milking, do the chores, get everything ready for the next morning, and I didn't get in the house for dinner till about 8 o'clock. That's how my brother and I were raised.

Good training for you, huh?

That's why triathlons are easy for me. A lot of people think it's a big deal. "Omigod! 9, 10, 12 hours!" What if you had to pitch hay, move bales and move sacks all day long? Milk cows at night and do the chores. I'd say 50% is diet anyway. You have to eat right.

What do you do about diet?

Well, most triathletes have found out you have to live on natural foods—a lot of fresh vegetables, fresh fruit and whole grains. You've gotta stay away from man-made processed shit, oil and grease, gravy and sauces, cream, cheeses. You've gotta keep the animal fats out of your diet.

Have you always done that?

I've been at that now for the last four years.

Do you eat meat?

No. But I do eat fish.

Do you stay away from dairy products?

No butterfat. I'm not saying stay away 100% but maybe 98% of the time. I go in a restaurant and they can give me all the French bread they want and I'll eat it but I won't touch the butter.

Do you eat dessert?

Oh, yeah. But, see, it's not an everyday thing. I treat myself on weekends and that's it.

What do you like about triathlons?

I like the fact that I don't have to stick to any damn schedule. I train as I want. If there's a day I'm supposed to run and I don't feel like running, I don't do it. I'll take a bike ride. A lot of triathletes say, "This is my day to run. I don't feel like running but I've got to get out there." I think that's why I've lasted so long. I do it as I feel.

Have you been injured?

No. See, I never push myself. I never run myself into an injury. I would never say, "It hurts but I've got to keep going." I was never that kind of person. I've seen a lot of injuries over the years. I've seen a lot of my friends get so competitive they get hung up on it. "I'm gonna finish no matter what." It's not worth it.

What's it like at the Ironman?

It's a happening. A lot of glamour. A lot of parties. People from all over the world. A lot of serious people there. Sometimes they are so serious it makes you wonder. They fly in and fly out. But I have a good time. I go with a couple of friends and our wives go too. We go a week ahead of time and we have a lot of fun. It's the Super Bowl of triathlons. □

Jack sprinting the last 100 yards of the 1983 Hawaii Ironman Triathlon

Herb Blanchard

Herb Blanchard has been a basketball coach for 24 years, coaching everything from 4th graders to his present job as varsity coach at McAteer High School in San Francisco. 1985 was a special year for Herb, as his team won the city championship. The S.F. Examiner *paid tribute to him with an article about himself and his career, but Herb replied: "Don't talk about me. Talk about the kids. They're the ones who did it."*

I met Herb at McAteer High and we sat in the gym and watched his team warm up as we talked. Only then did I learn about Herb's own outstanding track and field performances, both in college and now in the Master's division.

How much pressure is on a coach? Do you get ulcers or anything?

I don't get ulcers, but there is a lot of pressure. Most of it self-imposed; I mean I won't lose my job if we lose a game. All the coaches in S.F. are close personal friends. But you remember when you were a little kid, you wanted to beat your best friend most of all?

In the '50s, kids played a different sport each season. Is it still that way?

No. Out of this group here, there's only one kid who does anything but basketball. These kids play basketball year-round, summer leagues, the works. They get one month off.

Vital Statistics
Herb Blanchard, 47
Date of Birth: January 10, 1939
Born: Bossier City, Louisiana
Height: 5'7" **Weight:** 185 (temporarily)
Job: Basketball coach
Lives in: San Francisco, California
Activities: Running, weight training

It's like being professional, isn't it?

Yeah. I think they're probably missing something, but if you're gonna be good, you gotta do it this way.

You're around kids all the time. Have they changed since your high school days?

They're growing up too fast. Maybe it's television, the media, the pro sports scene. Kids won't sit on the bench now. If they're not first string, they don't want to be here. The peer pressure is different than it used to be. There's the drug scene and tight money now, too. You need money for clothes. It didn't matter if you didn't have clothes and stuff when I was in school.

All your players, except one or two, are black. Is that because of ability or desire?

It's a combination of things. One, the black athlete has been playing ball all his life. And two, they're the ones that don't have real good jobs. A lot of kids don't play sports if they have a good job.

Let's talk about you. Tell me about your track career.

I went to San Jose State on a track scholarship. I ran the 100, 220 and the 440.

How fast were you?

9.6 in the hundred, 20.8 in the 220, and 47.5 for the 440.

That's really fast. Did you work out with weights?

My college coach, Bud Winter, was really ahead of his time. We did weight training when it was considered unusual. He was also a great fan of relaxing and stretching. And the front runner theory: if you're out in front, he said, you control the race.

What happened after college?

I started running distance—easy, slow distance. When I turned 40, I started running Master's track. I ran for 3 years—running the 880, 1500 and mile.

How fast?

2:12 for the 880, and 4:57 for the mile. I'm proud of my personal record in the Bay to Breakers, too. 46 minutes and 30 seconds. It's a 6:15 mile pace for 7½ miles.

What are you doing nowadays?

Jogging about 25 miles a week. I'd like to get up to 50. I'd also like to lose about 20 pounds. I had a back problem, and in the last two years I've gained 30 pounds.

What do you eat?

All fattening foods. *(Laughter)* Poor diet right now. I know what I should be doing, I'm just not doing it. It's hardest during basketball season because of the stress. I have to eat on the run.

Other than the running itself, what do you like about Master's competiton?

Traveling and meeting people. And the social atmosphere where it doesn't matter what your economic background is. We have running in common. Later on you get to know that this guy is a doctor and that guy is a teacher. But at first, you're only concerned about your one common interest—running. □

Jack Fulton

They're growing up too fast. Maybe it's television, the media, the pro sports scene. Kids won't sit on the bench now.

Herb out running

Jack Fulton

Coaching his all-city championship basketball team, 1985

Bill Bullis

Bill Bullis, Dick Zanuck (see p. 144) and I used to rent a beachside cottage in Santa Cruz for $35 a month. Bill was a high school swimming champion from L.A., a strong ocean swimmer and a graceful surfer. He surfed in Santa Cruz in the '50s before the days of rubber suits and when boards were over 10 feet long. There were no surfing crowds then. Santa Cruz was a sleepy, slow-moving town where 40% of the people were retired and 60% of the land was owned by the church. Surfing was crude in those days compared to the technology, maneuverable lightweight boards and skill of surfers today. But the lack of crowds, the relatively few surfers and... the risk of freezing when you fell off your board in 50° water made it something special. For a few years Bill spent most of his weekends in Santa Cruz.

While at Stanford he worked out lifting weights in a gym and soon after he began his law practice in Los Angeles he began an early morning routine of running and weight training that he follows to this day. He still surfs in Santa Monica and Hawaii on vacations.

For this interview we met at the Santa Monica Beach Club and ran his usual five miles on the beach. Then we went to his gym near Westwood, which has a pool, squash and racquetball courts, aerobic dance classes and a weight lifting room with super equipment and, being L.A., baby... mirrors all around, colorful carpets and dozens of well-muscled, healthy looking guys and curvaceous, leotard-clad girls looking straight out of a tv commercial. We sat on a couch in the lobby and Bill, now 50, talked about his workout schedule while the hunks and babes walked by.

Vital Statistics
Bill Bullis, 50
Date of Birth: May 21, 1936
Born: Los Angeles, California
Height: 6'1" **Weight:** 170
Job: Lawyer
Lives in: Los Angeles, California
Activities: Running, weight training, surfing

What's your routine now?

Monday, Wednesday and Friday I get up about 4 o'clock. I drive down to the gym, park my car and run through the streets for about 45 minutes.

Why so early?

Because there's no smog, no traffic, and it's quiet. It's uncrowded. I have a good time. It's cool in the summer, sometimes a little cold in the winter. I even run in the rain. It doesn't bother me.

Isn't it dark then?

It's dark but you can see. Occasionally you have to be careful because of the ruts and things like that in the road. After I run, I'll go into the gym and do about 45 minutes on the Nautilus or free weights. I try to work each major muscle group. Before I used the Nautilus, I'd do squats, something for the calves, toe raises sometimes, situps, something for the shoulders like bench presses or handstand pushups. I don't use a lot of weight. And then something for the chest. I do pushups between benches or just bench presses. Maybe a military press of some kind. Then some leg-ups. But not heavy weights—high repetition, you know. The idea is to keep each muscle group active.

That is your own concoction?

My own. If you come into a gym and ask an instructor to do a program for you, it'll take you all day to do it. Four exercises for each thing and exercise the muscles you can't even see. So I just pared it down to where I work the major muscle groups.

What does all this do for you? Physically and mentally?

Well, physically it makes you feel good, and mentally it raises your spirits because you don't have to look at a fat slob in the mirror. You take out your aggressions. It also makes you a lot more energetic. Like if you're sluggish or pissed off or tired you go ahead and work out and although you're physically spent after your workout, mentally you're much more alert.

What do you do when you travel?

I bring shoes and run. I've run every place in the world. France, Hawaii, England.

Do you run in the cities?

Yes. In England, Hyde Park is great. Paris, along the Seine. Sometimes people look at you kind of funny. Then in Leningrad and in Bulgaria.

When you're traveling do you do anything besides running?

I do pushups and situps. I have a regular traveling routine. Also handstands up against the wall. Isometrics in a doorway.

How does it all work out with your family?

The only time it interferes is if my wife wants to go to a party and stay

Monday, Wednesday and Friday I get up about 4 o'clock.

Craig Griffith

Bill and two surfing companions in Australia.

up late. But as I get older I just figure I'll pick it up in the afternoon.

What do you eat?

I eat everything but not a lot. I avoid junk food. I just try to eat great food. I think the whole secret is to just eat when you're hungry. When I'm not hungry I'll just miss a meal. I find a lot of times when I'm working I'll get real busy and forget about eating. And suddenly it's three o'clock and I'll say, my God I've missed lunch. And go, well, it's too late; dinner's in another couple of hours.

Do you ever work out with somebody or do you generally do it alone?

I used to run with somebody. But you know I kind of like running alone. It's a time when you can think.

What do you think about?

It's a good time for solving problems. You can organize your day or if I have a trial I think about how I'm going to handle it.

What kind of work do you do in your law practice?

Well, general business. I'm doing less and less trial work.

How many days a week do you work and what hours?

Six days a week. Eight hours a day anyway.

So you put in 50 hours a week?

Oh yeah.

You going to keep doing this. Do you like it?

I'm unqualified to do anything else. *(Laughter)* Actually I enjoy it. It's more interesting than doing something routine or clerical. A fair amount of challenge to it. It's just that it's so time-consuming. It tends to eliminate a lot of other things I'd like to do.

Couldn't you work less?

Well, it's difficult. Everybody's looking for the kind of deal where they don't have to work that many hours.

What would you tell somebody who's just starting to work out? Or somebody who has started and is having trouble staying with it?

Well, first, working out by yourself is hard. So, go to a place where there are people that you like. Where, you know, everyone kids the other guys and says, "Where were you last week?" And Jesus, when you see sights like that *(good-looking woman in leotards walks by)*, it makes it worthwhile coming in here. *(Laughter)* Also just to do something that isn't burdensome or time-consuming or hard. Or such a chore or so painful that all you want to do is avoid it. Don't do it every day; you've got to take rests once in a while. Like when I go to Hawaii I just run once or twice but I don't do it regularly.

Back to problem solving. Do you just get out and start running and let things float into your mind?

No. Say I'm facing some kind of deadline. Like, the other day I had to give a speech. I was really dreading it. So I did my whole speech running. I just thought it out. And it was funny, when I got up to give the speech—there were 400 people there and I thought there were going to be 75—I had gone over it so many times I just did it without looking at any notes. And it came out pretty well.

Has that worked with problems? Do you think them out better when you're running?

I think so. It's the only time that I'm alone. If you're in the office, the phone is ringing, people are coming in and out, there's a hundred things you have to do. If you're home there's the kids, you know... When I'm out running there's nobody there to bug me. And another thing, I find I get so engrossed in thinking that when I run my five miles, it's over so quick I never even think about it being exercise. □

Mary Ann Buxton

Mary Ann Buxton competed in and completed the Hawaii Ironman Triathlon (2.4 mile ocean swim, 118 mile bike ride, 26.2 mile run) no less than five times. Her fastest time is 13:40. She's done the Ultimate Endurance Triathlon, several 50-mile races, a number of marathons. Last year she ran in the Western States 100, reputedly the world's toughest race–100 miles through the Sierras.

Mary Ann was formerly the Product Manager of Olympic Marketing at Levi-Strauss Co. and in charge of designing, manufacturing and outfitting the clothing worn by the Olympic athletes. She currently is setting up her own company–Racing Silks–to manufacture sports clothing and is a consultant for the Olympic Committee on Competitive Clothing.

Mary Ann's biggest fan (and coach) is her husband, Tom Barthold, himself an outstanding endurance athlete. On their honeymoon they went to Tahiti and ran in the Tahiti Marathon.

Vital Statistics

Mary Ann Buxton, 43
Date of Birth: June 13, 1942
Born: Guatemala
Height: 5'5" **Weight**: 122
Job: Owner, *Racing Silks* Sports Clothing Co., consultant, Olympic Committee on Competitive Clothing
Lives in: San Anselmo, California
Activities: Running, cycling, swimming

I started running when I turned 30 and thought I was really getting over the hill. I was always a chubby kid, but I was getting fatter.

I started running two miles every day. It felt so good. I was doing two miles a day when I came to Levi's and I thought that was a really long distance. Then I read about the Levi's Ride and Tie. I thought it would be fun to do. I could ride a horse to get my picture taken but I couldn't really *ride*. So I learned.

My first real race was the Dipsea. There were all the people looking so great and fit and I said, "This sport's for me." The Dipsea is such a high and such a beautiful place to run. It just captured me.

How did you get from there to the Ironman?

Well, I did the Ride and Tie, which at first looked impossible. It's about 40 miles total so I had to learn how to really ride a horse. I also had to learn to run at least 30 miles. Then once I did the S.F. Marathon, I thought, wow! I can do anything.

How fast did you run it?

3:30. I've never gotten any faster.

That's really good.

After that I ran a few more marathons, including Boston and New York. Then I read an article about the Ironman in *Sports Illustrated* and that just looked like the next challenge.

What did you do to train for it?

I had to learn to swim.

***Learn* to swim?**

I could swim but not efficiently. I'd done some small triathlons but I was using this Esther Williams breast-

David Epperson

Mary Ann on the bike leg of the 1983 Ironman Triathlon.

stroke. So I had to get a coach. She taught me an efficient long distance stroke.

How much did you train for that first one?

I trained for four months. I swam in the evenings four nights a week and cycled on the weekends. And ran a couple hours a day. I built up to training all day on the weekends, 8 hours a day doing some combination of the three sports.

All *day?*

You know when you're going that slow, it's like nothing. You go out for a 15-mile bike ride with a picnic in between and your day is gone.

What's a typical year for you in races?

Tom and I put a calendar up that has big enough spaces to put all our events on. We of course do the Ironman and Ride and Tie and the American River 50—that's 50 miles from Sacramento to Auburn, a real pretty run. And we've gotten into the habit of doing the Grand Canyon Double Run, 42 miles. Then we put a few marathons up there and just try to work them in.

What do you eat?

Lots. (Laughter) Too much. There's where Tom has made a real difference in my life because I used to eat just anything. Prepared foods. (I'll never give up corn chips, no matter what he says.) I gave up coffee and chocolate. And now I have carob . . . I live on carob covered almonds. *(Laughter)*

Do you see yourself as a role model for aspiring athletes?

Well, I have a kind of mission. I want people to see that I'm not a great athlete by any means, but that by determination and love of the sport, I can be involved in sports that to me and other people starting out look impossible.

I would hope that there are other women like me who feel they could have their lives enriched by sports. I've inspired some others to get up and run. They always end up passing me up. *(Laughter).* □

Gene Cohn

Levi's
80

Donn Carswell

Vital Statistics
Donn Carswell, 50
Date of Birth: February 4, 1936
Born: New York, New York
Height: 6'0" **Weight**: 220
Job: Civil engineer; owner, health club
Lives in: Lihue, Kauai, Hawaii
Activities: Racquetball, weight lifting, running, swimming, horse-back riding

Curly Carswell is a hard man to keep down. When his car went over a cliff in Wainha, Hawaii, Curly was knocked unconscious, but came to, climbed out, hitched home and went deep-sea fishing. Only a few days later did he discover he had a concussion. When he was an all-star guard on Stanford's football team in the '50s, he was hit from the side by a USC wingback and severely injured his knee, yet played in the Hula Bowl a few weeks later, until his knee collapsed and he went in for surgery. In his long athletic career, as football player, judo black belt, rodeo rider, and deep sea diver, Curly has survived accidents, injuries and pain that would have felled lesser mortals, including a separated shoulder, broken nose and ribs, and a smashed ankle. But the most serious challenge to his spirit and powers of recuperation came on New Year's Eve, 1982, when Curly was severely injured in a fireworks explosion in Princeville on the island of Kauai, Hawaii. He was struck on the back, arm and thigh with chunks of burning metal. "People said it looked like I had green flares all over my legs and back," he recalls.

Curly now owns and operates the state-of-the art Kauai Athletic

Club with 800 members. The club also administers a post-operative industrial accident program.

How did the accident happen?

I was putting on a fireworks show in Princeville because I had a powder license. And the fuse on an explosive the size of a volleyball was defective. There's a charge that kicks it out of a tube and moves it up about 1000 feet and about 4 seconds later, once it's kicked out of the tube, there's a second fuse that's ignited, then burns for about 4 seconds then it blows it up into the air. The thing went off right out of the tube. It was phosphorous and iron pyrex and it was like getting hit by a hand grenade. I was down and running because you always get showered with sparks. But had I been standing up I'd have got it all in the back. I took most of it in the leg.

The newspaper said they thought you'd never walk again, much less play racquetball.

I was in a hospital, in and out 5 times over two months. One piece went almost all the way through my thigh that they had to clean and clean and clean. They opened me up from stem to stern, all the way up from my knee to my buttocks. I had one operation here in Kauai and then they couldn't get any deeper. They were right next to the femoral artery so they closed me up, shipped me into Honolulu and I was at Queen's Hospital down there for about 3 weeks.

A lot of pain through all that.

Oh yeah, it was interesting. I've got a high tolerance for pain though, I

Curly with Brownie troop on wagon ride on Kauai, Hawaii

I thought I'd never walk again. Feeling real sorry for myself. Then suddenly I got this real uplift.

guess. I've always been dinged up, problems in football and other sports. I had a judo match in the Marines and the guy threw me and separated my shoulder. I got so mad I went in with one arm and finished him off, broke three of his ribs. I have a left knee which was wiped out in the Stanford/USC game in 1956, for which I got the game ball. It was a chop block; to this day I believe it was set up and intentional.

So what did you do to recover from the fireworks accident?

I went through this thing rather stoically in the rehab phase and felt real positive about regaining my former condition. The fact that you've been in good shape all your life and have a positive mental attitude and you don't feel sorry for yourself, you're just going to get up and get out. My doctor knew how much I hated being in the hospital. He came down one day and said, "You're going home this afternoon at 3." I went on the plane in a wheelchair and I swore—you know, my wife was going to meet me—that I was going to walk off. So I walked off on crutches and padded down the steps and then I recouped at home with the help of my wife and her cousin who is a nurse. Then I had something happen, one of those almost mystical religious happenings. I was feeling at the lowest ebb ever, like 7:30 one morning. Feeling low and dejected, I thought I'd never walk again. Feeling real sorry for myself. Then suddenly I got this real uplift. Like something was happening that made me feel good. It turned out that there was. There is a Unity Church in Honolulu and one on Maui and those two churches at that time were saying a prayer for us *(Curly's brother-in-law was injured in the same explosion).*

My brother-in-law was standing just 200 feet away. It just missed killing him because it missed a nerve and an artery on one hand. He is still partially disabled in his left arm. He was much worse off than I was during that period. He was really down, had a lot of additional surgery and they had to graft and redirect some of his muscles and change tendons around . . . I got off pretty easy.

I had another operation where they did some grafts to close up the last of the wounds. After that, I started walking on the beach, then jogging and just bringing the muscles back. Then I started doing a lot of Nautilus work. I went down to the fitness center in Poipu. And started working out there and then I got a line of my own Nautilus equipment and moved it up here.

I got very interested in racquetball; I've always been a handball player. We never had any courts on the island and I started to look around, looking at clubs, thinking about maybe putting one in Princeville. So we zeroed in on this piece of ground. This has been a genesis since before the hurricane in November of 1982.

What did that do?

Pretty well flattened the island. Wiped out all the gyms, the high schools, wiped out the other fitness center. Things were just chaotic on Kauai. Everybody was rebuilding, roofers were having a field day. In January I got a second line of Nautilus. February 7th I opened in a little drugstore and put in the equipment. I had a dance floor and we made a couple of little locker rooms and put a Jacuzzi in the back and we opened. There was nothing else available on the island and that filled the need. We operated like that for over a year.

I'd been looking at clubs and playing racquetball every chance I had. My idea was to have a full service club, not just one specialized thing. Racquetball kind of peaked and then maybe it declined a bit. Everywhere you went you'd see somebody converting racquetball courts to aerobics, because they wanted to diversify.

My goal has been to establish an effective post-operative or post-industrial accident rehab program, which we have done. We work with the Kauai medical group and the therapist is right next door. We bring the guys in and we start them through. There's expertise and there's guidance. It used to be the guy that was a construction worker and had broken his ankle—after the rehab, he'd just go back off and start doing construction. Nowadays they actually get the guy out there and they teach him how to lift the wheelbarrow, how to pick up something safely, how to hammer a nail safely, how to turn. They run through this industrial program. Hawaii 15 years or 20 years ago when we came here, hell, we had an old wooden floor in the dispensary and a general practitioner who would treat people, give them three aspirins, throw them out and tell them to come back the next day. Half the time they didn't. Ours is a totally refined situation. We take basic measurements, measure the body fat, do a profile on them, and refer them to a diet/nutritional

counselor. We set them up on a Nautilus and free weight program and we monitor. We have an instructor with them every time they work out, one on one. It takes a little bit more effort, but the most important thing is motivation and supervision to keep them going and pretty soon they pick up the lifestyle.

Our philosophy in the club is also very strong on youth. Being aware that in certain clubs they exclude kids—you know, they bring dirty footprints and noise and all that—we are a family-oriented club and we want the kids in here. We have a high school membership and they can come in between 2:30 and 4:30. They pay 20 bucks a month, no initiation and they get to use the weights and everything else. We're also trying to get a junior league started in racquetball and we have a family membership this year. If you have a kid that's 14 and under and you've a couple membership or a joint membership, the kid gets in free if he is with his parents. A working mother that wants to come here and work out pays a buck for babysitting and she can take a class and not have to worry about the kid. Obviously the future of this club lies in the youth of Kauai, the future members.

What do you do now?

A lot of handball, racquetball, swimming. I try to do my Nautilus and free weight workout three times a week. Horseback riding.

You still get into rodeos?

My kids do more of that now. I do a bit. I rope. I used to get into steer wrestling and all that but my wife made me back off. □

Marlene Cimons

L.A. Times

Marlene Cimons is a general assignment reporter for the Los Angeles Times, *working in Washington, D.C. She covers politics and anything associated with Washington. She also does free-lance magazine articles on running and other sports, and covered the 1984 Olympic Marathon and track and field events for the* Times. *She took up running herself in 1980.*

I had a friend who was running a marathon and I stood around to watch. I was captivated by the faces of the people when they finished, this sense of accomplishment and achievement, and pain that they seemed to be experiencing. And I said to myself, "A year from now I'm going to run my first marathon." That people would be willing to test themselves to that extent was a very inspiring thing for me. I wondered whether or not I would be willing to do that.

When did you start training for a marathon?

About five months after I started running.... I used to go to this aerobics class, then one day the classes were cancelled. I had found the classes kind of boring, yet I got addicted to the point where I wanted exercise every day. So when the classes were cancelled, I was going crazy wanting to do something. I put on a pair of sneakers–that's all I had–and went out and ran for ten minutes. I'd never done it before in my life; I was 35 years old. And I loved it. Runner's high. First time.

So you got enthused about running?

The next day I went out and bought a pair of running shoes. The first week I went out and ran a mile every day. The next week it was two miles every day. The week after that, three miles. After six weeks, I had built up to four or five miles a day. I'm a classic Type A personality. Overdoing it is my biggest problem. Now I do 75-80 miles a week, when I could probably do quite well on 50-mile weeks, go in rested and run a faster time. But I'm compulsive.

When do you run?

Well, I trained for my last marathon while covering a presidential campaign. I did a lot of traveling with Bush and Ferraro, attempting to run in strange cities on the road, which is no picnic. You end up getting up at 4 o'clock in the morning and if you don't know your way around the city, or it's sort of inner city where you're staying, you end up coming back to the hotel and running the block around the hotel for an hour and 12 minutes just to get your time.

With the Vice Presidential candidates, there's always Secret Service and local cops stationed right at the hotel. I told them as I was going out (this was in Dayton or Akron, Ohio), "I'm going to circle this hotel for about an hour. If you don't see me after a minute or two comin' around come look for me." And they'd sort of nod and wave. It looked like they were getting dizzy and nauseous watching me. But you have to do things like that if you really want to train.

When you're at home, do you run alone?

I used to be a very solitary runner, but now I've hooked up with a group. I run virtually every day now with a group of guys. We all meet at six o'clock in the morning. And I have to run about 1½ miles to get there. They run about 7 miles and I end up running about 10 or 11. I'm not sure why I enjoy it so much; I never thought I could run with a group. I always thought I needed to be alone. But I run every day and they run only 5 days a week so I get to be alone the other two days. The other thing I like is that, on the whole, they run 20-30 seconds faster a mile, which I can do if pushed.

And I love these guys. They're terrific, wonderful to be with. One of the guys is blind. And it's the most extraordinary thing. This guy is such an inspiration–I shouldn't even say this because he'd think it was patronizing–but a couple of times on the run we have to stop to walk a few steps simply because the sidewalk space is not enough for him to be able to maneuver. He's got two shoelaces tied together and he loops one end around his arm and one end around one of us to guide him. We have to stop sometimes to move up a curb or something like that. So every time

Vital Statistics
Marlene Cimons, 40
Date of Birth: March 13, 1945
Born: Yonkers, New York
Height: 5'6" **Weight**: "I haven't weighed myself in 5 years."
Job: Reporter
Lives in: Bethesda, Maryland
Activities: Running, cycling, cross country skiing

I went out and ran for ten minutes. I'd never done it before in my life, I was 35 years old. And I loved it! Runner's high. First time.

we stop I turn my watch off. When we start again I turn it on and it beeps every time. He keeps telling me, "You're really sick. You're the sickest runner I ever met." *(Laughter)*

When you are running alone, are you doing some writing in your head as you run?

Oh, all the time. On the days when I'm alone, yeah. On the days when I'm with these guys, we talk about news. It's a great cultural exchange. We talk about books we're reading, movies we've seen. And I love that. I really do. So I don't feel I've sacrificed anything. My psyche doesn't seem to have suffered. I was curious about that because I thought maybe I'd be antsy and feel like I wasn't getting time by myself, but that hasn't happened.

Sounds like a great group.

Oh, it's a wonderful group. There are two doctors, one lawyer, another reporter. I met him running on the campaign trail and he said, "You oughta run with my group." And that's how I got into it. I'm the first woman. They call me the Geraldine Ferraro of their running group because I've opened doors for women that will never be closed again. *(Laughter)*

If there weren't the races, you'd still be running, right? What difference do the races make?

Truly, the only time I feel good in a race is when it's over. I'm all uptight when I go down there. I say to myself, "Why am I doing this?" I sort of hate it while it's going on because I don't feel good. The only time I really feel good is when I cross the finish line and the time is an improvement. When that happens I feel *so* good—that's why I do it. It's such a great feeling.

Why do I run marathons? There's something about just doing it. About accomplishing it. My first marathon was 3:53, my second marathon was 2 minutes slower. They were both in New York and that's why. Running New York is absolutely the most wonderful experience of your life. But if you want to run a fast time, don't count on New York. I still felt good after the second marathon, even though there was no improvement; I still felt like I had accomplished something terrific. And then the third one, of course, was that tremendous one I ran with Jeff (Galloway, author of *Galloway's Book on Running,* see page 54). Never in my life will I have another race like that.

I ran a 3:44 with Jeff and felt terrific. A year later, after a year of much better running in shorter distances, I ran a 3:46 marathon and felt terrible. I mean I felt terrible the whole day. I was tired. I had covered a campaign, I had been away most of the summer covering the Olympics. The fact that I ran as well as I did, and the fact that I ran consistently between 8:30 and 8:40 the whole time—I didn't slow down the last 8 miles or the last 10K—I ran 8:30 and 8:40 the whole time, it's because I did those long, long, long runs. I think this teaches your body to be consistent.

This is how Galloway changed your running?

The biggest change—when I listened to him was to extend the long run. You can read that in his book. To extend that long run to beyond marathon distance. I really was very hesitant about that at first because I thought if I ran 26 miles in training I would wipe myself out. But the truth is you don't run 26 miles in training the way you would run it in an actual marathon. I did plenty of 26+ mile training runs and felt fine enough to go out and run another 9 or 10 miles the next day. Because I ran them slowly enough.

So he turned out to be absolutely right. People just haven't caught on. They think the idea of running more than 26 miles is absurd.

Then do you taper off before a marathon?

A little bit. But I still run every day. Maybe instead of running 10 miles, the very last week I'll run like 3-5 every day, including the day before.

Have you ever, as an experiment, taken a couple of days off?

Are you kidding? That's blasphemy. *(Laughter)*

I can just hear Jeff arguing with you, about resting a day or two because your muscles would be so fresh that way. You tear a muscle down and the only thing that allows it to rebuild stronger is that day of rest.

I know. I know everything you say is true and everything that Jeff says is true. And I don't know what compels me not to listen. *(Laughter)* The thing is I tell myself that he's right. I tell myself, "I'd love to get some fast race times." But I say to him, "Jeff, if I rest, if I don't run, I'm not burning calories and I'll get really fat." He says, "Well, don't eat!" □

Peter Cole

Peter Cole has been surfing for 40 years. At age 55, he lives on the beach of the world's greatest surfing spot, Oahu's North Shore, with his wife Sally and their two children. When the surf is up, Peter will spend 12-14 hours a week in the water. Peter's favorite surfing spot is Sunset Beach, where the waves always break like an avalanche, or when it gets bigger than 20 feet, at Waimea Bay.

Last winter I went to Hawaii and did some interviews. Peter, who I hadn't seen since the '50s, was the first person I visited. A tropical storm was just starting to blow as I walked up to his house. He opened the door (looking remarkably like I remembered him), handed me a beer, got out the corn chips and we sat down and talked about the intricacies of big wave riding and powerful "water men" Peter had known. Peter was exactly the same–same enthusiasm, same infectious energy, same slightly out-of-control humor and zest for life. The surfing revolution hadn't changed his style, outlook or the shape of his board one iota. He got out his "scrapbook"–a shoe box of dog-eared big wave photos–and talked about the old days and the new days.

Peter was born in Los Angeles and grew up in Santa Monica. At 14, he started surfing at Malibu. At Stanford he was an outstanding swimmer: he swam the 1500 meters in 18:47. He moved to Hawaii in 1958 and he's been there ever since. Peter is a mathematical statistician and designs and develops computer programs. He goes to work at 6:30 each morning so he can leave early in the afternoon to hit the surf.

After talking we went outside to shoot a picture of Peter and his board. The storm was really blowing now. I stood in the rain, trying to protect the camera with an umbrella that kept collapsing in the wind, to Peter's great glee. When we finished I walked to my car, Peter following me. "Hey, how is it at Sunset today?" "About 6-8 feet," I replied. Peter started moving fast. He was, for probably the three-thousandth time, and in the classic surfing sense, "stoked." He ran for his board and as I drove down the road he was tugging at the door of his car like an 18-year-old in his second year of surfing–heading once again for Sunset Beach.

Vital Statistics
Peter Cole, 55
Date of Birth: October 12, 1930
Born: Los Angeles, California
Height: 6'2" **Weight**: 195
Job: Computer assistant analyst
Lives in: Sunset Beach, Oahu, Hawaii
Activities: Surfing, swimming

What kind of board do you use?

A semi-gun, about 10 feet long. Then I have an 11'6" board for bigger waves. And they're the same shape I used when I came over here in '58.

When did they start riding bigger waves over here?

At Makaha as early as '50-'51.

What's the attraction at Waimea?

When it gets big and it's just a washing machine along this whole north shore, it's deep there and you can usually get out in the channel. It's the safest big wave you can ride. You can just sit there and say, "Is that big enough?" And you might take it and then it gets a little bigger. Everything is perfect. And it always reaches the point where you chicken out because it's just too big, just too much water.

How does that compare with Sunset and Pipeline?

You probably get more power from a 12 ft. wave at those two places than anywhere else in the world. But when it gets beyond 12 ft., you can't really ride there. Now Waimea is lousy between 12 and 20. Over 20, it gets a longer line to it, and it's just a totally different dimension. When Waimea closes down and becomes totally unmanageable, then surfers go to Makaha which will be 20+. That happens once every 2 or 3 years. That's probably the ultimate of big wave riding.

Are all the guys who ride 20 ft. waves real good swimmers? What qualities do you need?

Most of the guys over the years have been good water men. Like José Angel. Jim Fisher was great in the water. Rod Lundquist, Buzzy Trent, Rick Grigg are good swimmers. Nowadays with a leash, a lot of guys do well without being good swimmers.

Why the leash?

The leash keeps them from having to swim.

They wear the leash in big waves?

Oh, yeah. They're wearing leashes at Waimea.

Is it dangerous?

I think it's dangerous. I would refuse to wear one. In big waves it's 12-25 ft. in length so that it's safer. But if the

My goal is to be riding Sunset when I'm 69.

McGillivary & Freeman

Peter at Sunset Beach, 1978

Ask any of the old time surfers about funny stories and they'll invariably start with one about Peter Cole. Fred Van Dyke (see p. 124) tells the story about when Peter first arrived in Hawaii and was teaching math at Punahou High School. The kids were thrilled to have a teacher who surfed and "they would follow us to the beach on weekends. So at Alo Moana the wind's blowing about 20 mph offshore. Peter's checking the waves. He takes his contact lenses out because he wants to go surfing and one of them blows in the wind. So he's got all of the kids looking for the contact lens on the ground. He finally says, 'No, no, no. I've got a better idea.' So he grabs his other contact lens and lets it blow in the wind. He says, 'Now look for it where it blew.' Lost both of them. The kids are looking at him, 'This is my math teacher?! This guy gets paid?' There's kids who've graduated—that was 25 years ago—who still talk about that. Peter Cole and his contact lenses."

My total exercise is surfing.

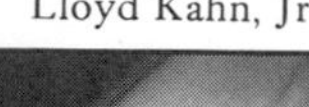

Lloyd Kahn, Jr.

Why is this man laughing and why is this picture blurred? Because the wind has just blown away the photographer's umbrella and he's falling backward. Peter Cole and his 10 foot 1950 Ford model "semi-gun" surfboard, sans leash.

board gets caught broadside on a real big wave, it could drag you down to the bottom. I would rather just be on my own. I don't want to be tied to any surfboard.

Has there been an evolution of people riding big waves?

Oh, yes. There are so many good surfers. When we first came over here, there might have been a dozen that really rode well. Now there are hundreds that just tear the place apart, doing things that were unheard of in our day. But in big waves there's not much difference between the old days and now. Because on a big wave, you're not going to be doing much hot dogging. A big wave is an equalizer. Everybody goes back to the long board, more weight, a conventional shape. Not a lot of performing. They're just trying to get a big wave.

How long a board do these guys use?

They're starting to think about 12 ft. board lengths. But most of the guys who are riding consistently, go about 10 ft., 9'6" to 10'6".

Have you tried the tri-fins?

No. I haven't changed since 1945. I use a single fin. I surf basically the same style. Age 54 is not the time to go switching to something new. I surf all the time—at Sunset. Sometimes Waimea. But I'm much more conservative now and I'll sit until it's not crowded. And I'll get maybe 2 or 3 waves.

Do you mind being on waves with other people?

Yeah. I don't like being on a big wave with anybody. Unless I'm familiar with who it is and I'm on the inside. And these guys are pulling off so far in and so far over to where I want to be at my age, that I can't ride outside of them.

You can't be on the outside of them?

It's a totally different style. In my day, I liked to sit way outside, see the wave coming, have a long board, bicycle into it, and have a gradual drop down into it and come around. They, with their smaller boards, will sit way inside of where I am. We end up at the same spot but I'm going into an obstacle course and they're just taking off on my left, on my right. My concentration gets thrown off. I end up pulling off. The only good waves I've had lately have been where I lucked out and I was the only one in a line-up.

All these years is that basically what you've done to keep in shape?

Surfing has been it, from the end of September to the end of April. I swim a lot because I don't use a leash. I lose my board, I swim. So my total exercise is surfing. When there isn't surf I swim about 1200 meters, 3 days a week. And that's it. I try to keep my weight down by not pigging out. But I do not like exercise for exercise sake.

How much do you surf during a month?

When there's good surf, I'll get in at least 3 times during the week, in the afternoon, for 2-6 hours. Then I'll go in for 4 hours on Saturday and Sunday.

McGillivary & Freeman

Peter Cole in classic photo of 25-30 foot wave at Waimea Bay in the late '50s. Peter rode all the way across the wave, but white water eventually caught him.

Do you think you'll be surfing forever?

Oh, yeah. My goal is to be riding Sunset when I'm 69. I'll probably have a short duration left for Waimea. For 20 ft. waves I'm probably reaching almost the limit where I'm going to have to think twice about it.

Why?

Well, the crowd, and I'm too conservative. To ride that kind of surf you work on instinct. Now I'm thinking too much. "Jeez, that wave looks big." Where when I was younger I didn't even think about it. I just took off. Now I think about the crowd. I make excuses. I will take off but everything has to be right. And the chances of having that exactly right, primo condition are slim. I'm riding poorly these days at Waimea. Sunset I have no qualms. I feel as comfortable and relaxed riding it as I ever did.

On big waves, what happens when you get caught by white water?

Once you get down to the bottom and you come across and you ride the wave, you hit the deep water. The big part of the wave is over and it flattens out. At the very end the white water will catch up to you and you'll lose momentum and speed because you're in the deep water. It'll get choppy. You just fall off. The whole ride is over.

What happens if you fall from the top?

Oh, you get a terrible wipe-out. Just an immense wipe-out. You bounce. You go down into the depths. You get jarred around. People have ruptured their disc. I herniated my disc in 1980. My brother's had 3 ruptured discs—he's had to quit surfing. He's had some wipe-outs you wouldn't believe.

But you still get the same thrill as always from surfing, don't you?

Oh, yeah. I enjoy surfing as much now and do as much of it as I ever did. If I hear the surf is good and I don't make it, I'm depressed. □

Andy Crow

A familiar and provocative sight at marathons in northern California is a runner wearing a top hat, carrying a cane and wearing a t-shirt that reads "Get Rolfed by Andy Crow." Usually at about the 20-mile mark, when most of the racers are beginning to wonder if it was worth it, the top-hatted figure starts doing some deep-tissue manipulation for selected stragglers. Invariably, those runners feel better, perk up and carry on in greatly improved condition to finish the race.

Andy Crow is a senior rolfer who specializes in working with athletes. Andy is also an athlete himself. In his 50th year, he ran 7 marathons, 9 Bud Light triathlons and the Ironman.

Andy and I went to high school in San Francisco together in the '50s. Then I lost track of him for over 30 years. Last year, bothered with a nagging groin injury from running, I asked Harry Hlavac, the Mill Valley podiatrist, for advice. "I'd go see Andy Crow," he said. Sure enough, here was Andy, all these years later, one of the country's top rolfers.

I'd heard rolfing was painful, but since I knew Andy I decided to give it a try. It consisted of 10 sessions of very deep... manipulation isn't the word, massage isn't either... rolfing! *There was* pain, *fairly intense maybe half a dozen times during each session, but I came to realize as the process unfolded that the pain had always been there, locked up in my body and in old scar tissue, and Andy was releasing it. He loosened up parts of my body that had been tight for decades. After the first session my rib cage was so expanded I could breathe much deeper. Andy would tell me where I'd been injured. "You fell on your shoulder here.... You've been hit hard just to the right of your spine here once.... You've cracked these two ribs." And I'd remember, yes, I landed on my shoulder falling off a bike two years ago, I got hit in the back with my surfboard 6 years ago, I cracked my ribs surfing about 20 years ago....*

Vital Statistics

Andy Crow, 50
Date of Birth: June 1, 1935
Born: San Francisco, California
Height: 5'8" **Weight**: 145
Job: Senior Rolf practitioner
Lives in: Sausalito, California
Activities: Running, swimming, cycling, diving

Rolfing is a process of anatomical organization through which the whole line of the body is brought into greater conformity with the line of gravity. So that the larger field of energy, which is gravity, will support and uplift the smaller field of gravity which is man. Rolfing balances the human body in gravity. And when a body is in perfect balance, it can't support stress and strain and imbalance and disease. So you're going to have more energy. You're going to improve total body efficiency.

Now, structure changes form and form changes structure. So if we go in and take a structure and we change the formation of it, the pattern of it, it will begin to operate differently. When this happens, it will further change that structure. It's an ongoing process.

How do you change the structure?

We change the myofascial system, which is everything in the body that's not bone, muscle and organ.

It's the covering of the muscles?

Of everything. It holds and shapes and positions the muscle; it holds and shapes and positions the bones, the organs, all the fluids, all the containers, all the vessels.

Is scar tissue myofascia?

Scar tissue is part of the fascial system in that it is the main protein of the body called collagen and is laid down under trauma and then begins to thicken and become more dense and fibrous, causing immobility rather than mobility.

So a lot of what you're doing is breaking up that scar tissue?

A lot of what we're doing is untying those parts of the body that are stopping you from moving in a proper, appropriate pattern. We're working on the body structurally while acupuncturists work on it through the meridians. People get rolfed and then go back to their acupuncturist, who is thrilled to see how the pulses now are really alive and moving where before they were blocked and constricted.

Do you specialize in athletes?

Yes, and children with structural problems. But I'll work with anybody. I'm a pioneer in my field. I worked more closely with Dr. Rolf than just about anybody in the country. I travelled with her for 8 months teaching other rolfers.

The body is like a vessel for all its experience. And mankind loves, for some reason, to hang onto its negativity.

You worked with her and had her work on you?

Well, we'd work in the day and at night I'd sit and read to her. Then we'd do research. I'd work on her and she'd work on me. Wonderful woman. She was a genius. See, a genius is one who sees simple answers to complex problems. She would say, "People are just treating symptoms. Structure has to do with cause. If you change the shape of the structure, then you can affect and eliminate causal relationships."

What does rolfing do for runners?

Something that nothing else can do. We can work on specific performance parameters immediately. I can take a runner and see where he is not moving to his optimum ability, then go in there and change that structure so it operates appropriately. See, a muscle is supposed to move individually and independently from its neighbor. It's not supposed to have to drag the neighbor around. Muscles should work individually and collectively *in concert* to perform a movement. Movement is nothing more than a relationship of physics. And physics is concerto, it's concert, it's harmonics. The body is suppposed to move harmoniously. It's supposed to move with the maximum efficiency and the least amount of restriction.

What about better lung capacity in rolfing?

In the very first session we increase the size of the thoracic cavity so it moves properly, to increase vital capacity. From that session on, your physiology is self-cleaning. In other words, every time you take a breath you're getting more oxygen than you got before . . .

Do you want to say something about pain?

The truth is that when people walk through the door, their bodies are in a state of being pain-full. And each time they leave, they are more pain-empty. Sometimes I'll touch something and the person will say, "My God, it's sore in there." But then we'll go back and visit that place later. Now after rolfing, this place that was dead is now alive. It had no circulation and now it does. The guy will say, "How come you're not working as deep as you used to? There's no pain now. Why?" Because now it's healthy and before it wasn't.

So you're releasing pain that's there already.

The body is like a vessel for all its experience. And mankind loves, for some reason, to hang onto negativity. Pain is just an expression of that negativity.

You grew up in San Francisco.

I'm a 5th generation San Franciscan. Isn't that disgusting?

5th generation? They were back there in the gold rush.

Before. My family were the most scurrilous, rotten bastards to ever come to the city. I mean it. I'm serious. *(Laughter)* My great-great-grandfather owned the first 3 whorehouses in San Francisco. *(Laughter)* And then he and his miserable son went into the shanghai business. Then went to China and started a yellow slave business. *(Laughter)* That's the truth. And in Chinatown in both San Francisco and Los Angeles started more whorehouses. More gambling.

Where did they come from?

Crow is Scottish-Irish. My family came here from Scotland as feudal lords runs out of Scotland at the end of the feudal period about 40 years before the Pilgrims. It's true. I saw the family castle—what was left of it—in Scotland, between Edinburgh and Aberdeen. They tore it down to chase the Crows out. *(Laughter)* I'm the humanitarian in the family.

You were a swimmer in high school?

Yeah. Swam morning, noon and night.

What events? Do you remember your times?

The 50 and 100 yard freestyle. My best 50 time was 23:01. I think I once broke 50 seconds in the 100.

Any other sports in high school?

I used to do trick riding in rodeos. Roll-overs and headstands and swing off the saddle and hang under the horse. But when I was 13 I broke my arm. In fact I used to play a helluva piano. But all that stopped with the arm, and I just went totally into swimming. This all got started when I was 4½ years old and my grandfather was William Randolph Hearst's private photographer . . . we would travel around the country interviewing famous people. So I got to sit on the lap of, either shake hands with or be picked up by, every

I was having this mad love affair with these 3 dolphins.

famous person on the face of the globe between 1938 and 1947. With the exception of Mussolini, Hitler . . . .

Like who?

Oh, Roosevelt, Truman, Babe Ruth, Joe Dimaggio . . . . He knew everybody, I mean everybody. My mother didn't believe in babysitters and she liked to do things so my grandfather took care of me. So anyway, I'm 4½ years old, it's the '39 World's Fair and Johnny Weismuller is the most famous swimmer in the world and we go over to interview him. I'd been to see the Tarzan films so, of course, Weismuller is my hero. So there I am, sitting on his lap. And he says to me, "Can you swim?" And I say, "No." He says, "My son can swim." I say, "How old is he?" "He's 3." And I say, "Well, I'm a big boy. I'm 4 and he's only 3." "Yes, but he can swim," Weismuller says, "When's your birthday?" I say, "June the first." He says, "That's *my* birthday." That just freaked me out. So every time I broke one of his records, I sent him a telegram. I broke every one of his world records except one.

You set a world record?

No, I beat his world record. Everybody did it though. All his records were shattered by 1936.

What are you going to do after you do all those marathons and triathlons this year, give up racing?

I'm going to give up everything and become fat and boozy. *(Laughter)* No, I will continue to swim about 2 miles a week and run anywhere from 10 to 70 miles a week. Right now, I also bicycle anywhere between 10 and 100 miles a week depending on my time.

Tell me that story about you and the dolphins in Florida.

Well, I was at the Ocean Reef Club, where they have a group of dolphins living in a lagoon; they put on a show. One of their tricks is, the trainer will ask someone in the audience for a quarter or a nickel, he'll show it to the dolphin, then throw it in the water and she'll retrieve it. That day no one had any coins, so I gave him my good luck piece, a solid silver poker chip I'd won in Monte Carlo in 1960. The trainer threw it in the water. The dolphin took off and came back with a nickel. She kept going out and coming back, but not with the coin. So after the show, the trainer, he knew I was a diver, said that I could go down and look for the coin. So in between shows for a couple of days I went diving. The dolphins were naturally curious about me, and I started having a wonderful time with them.

You're diving with a lung or something?

No, I can free dive about 70 or 80 feet so I can stay under the water for a couple minutes at a time without too much trouble. The dolphins were having such a good time fooling around that they'd stir up the bottom and I never did find it. But as it ended up, about the 4th day, I was having this mad love affair with these 3 dolphins. They would swim under my arms and raise me to the top and pull me around. I would grab onto their dorsal fin and they'd scoot down the side with me. It was incredible. I didn't want to leave. I was ready to leave my wife and run away with a dolphin. *(Laughter)*

Describe the ride the dolphin gave you.

One dolphin kept swimming up and looking me right in the eye. I would touch her and she would swim away and my hand would slide down her body. It was very exotic. Erotic, I should say. She would shimmer and shake and just go crazy. So I'm wondering, "What next, Crow?" Anyway, I'd come to the surface and I'm looking about 70 yards down the lagoon at this place where they're working with the dolphins and all of a sudden my arm floats up and there's this dolphin under my arm. She turns around and looks at me and my hand rests on her dorsal fin and she takes off. She pulls me a few feet and I let go, because I didn't know what she wanted to do. And she backs up. So I grabbed her fin with both hands and we *shot* 70 yards–better than water skiing. I mean I was planing out of the water. The only thing that was touching the water was my chest and my shorts. I'm just holding on with my hands and she's flying. I didn't even feel her tail. She's bottoming out and we're going about 25 miles an hour. She stops and I jump onto the raft. I start to take my fins off and all of a sudden, flop! She jumps up next to me. It was very exciting. I hated to leave.

What's in the future? What do you look forward to?

For years I've tried to have all my swimmers run and bicycle, and all my bicyclers swim and run, and all my runners, swim and bicycle. Consequently, I really like triathlons. I like the triathlete body. Triathlons

Jack Fulton

Andy Crow runs marathons with top hat, cane and t-shirt saying "Get Rolfed by Andy Crow."

produce a very well-balanced body, top to bottom, front to back. Most swimmers are overpowered on the top half, most runners are overpowered on the bottom. And the triathlete has this very nice balance. As does the decathlon champion. And I think that's the coming thing in sports.

How old can people be when they come to you?

My youngest patient was 3 hours old, a newborn baby with a misshapen crania. The oldest child I've ever worked on was 94 years. *(Laughter)* He was extraordinary. I should have paid *him* for everything I learned from him. When you live to be 94, you've learned how to survive in our times. That's the biggest error we have in our culture, we do not honor the wisdom of the old. In the Orient the most valued person in the village is the oldest one alive. In our culture we create senility.

Anyway, this man arrived here from Finland to see a geriatric physician, and he called me up and said, "I read article on plane. I all bent over. I not as tall, I not as strong and vigorous as I am when I young. You rolf me and make me young and handsome." I said, "Sure, c'mon in." And away we went. By the time we finished he was having an affair with a 47-year-old waitress.

Any other older people?

Well, I rolfed 3 ladies. They were 79, 81 and 83. By the time we finished, they all ran away with younger men. The 83-year-old came to me about the 6th session. She said, "I want you to help me. I consider you to be a very good friend." I said, "Gertrude, thank you." She said, "I have a problem and I'd like your advice on it." I said, "Great." She said, "Well, for the past month or so I've had strong desires to be with a man." And the way she said it was like, "How do I make it go away?" And I said to her, "Well, that's terrific. Good for you. What are you doing about it?" She said, "I don't know what you mean." I said, "Why don't you go get yourself a boyfriend?" And it was like I'd hit her with a flat iron. It had never occurred to her that was a viable possibility. She said, "A boyfriend?!" I said, "Sure. A good lookin' lady like you? Go out and get yourself a boyfriend." So she comes back in 2 weeks. And she says, "I took your advice." I said, "Well, that's great. Tell me about him." She says, "Well, his name is Daniel," and she blushes a little. "He's 71." I said, "Well, good for you, you dirty old lady. How do you like these younger men?" She said, "Well, he's wonderful. And besides that he can still . . . " She blushes, and I say, "He can still get it on?" She says, "Yes. That's it." I said, "My congratulations to you both." So they ran away to Canada together. The youngest gal, she runs away with a fella who's in his 60's. They go to Mexico. They're having a wonderful time down there. The middle one is a riot. She calls me about once a year. She calls herself the happy harlot of Leisure World (you're not going to be able to publish this). She says, "I could be a rich woman now. All these old farts want to marry me." (That's the way she talks) "You don't know what a good girl, how ethical, I've become." I said, "How ethical have you become?" She says, "All I have to do is marry these old farts, fuck 'em to death and collect on the insurance." *(Laughter)* "Joyce, gimme a break will ya?" She just laughs. I mean, she's *alive!* □

Pat Cunneen

Gary Stubbs

Pat Cunneen is a good-looking Irishman, a native San Franciscan, who has run a 3:01 marathon and a 38-minute 10K, runs in races whenever he can, often cycles 70 miles in a day with friends, has swum in the annual (chilly) Golden Gate swim the past 15 years, takes his kids backpacking, goes surfing and manages to keep all this going while serving as a full time S.F. fireman and part time engraver.

Pat's been running long enough to have given up marathons, no longer looks at his watch on training runs and doesn't follow a rigid training schedule. "I just try to get up a sweat every other day...." Recently he's started competing in triathlons and finished third in his age group in the Berkeley Iron Horse.

He started running in the early '60s, before running was such a rage. His wife Betty and their three children also run and the family was on the cover of Runner's World *in 1973. Pat is the Running Commissioner at the South End Rowing Club.*

Health and vigor seem natural in Pat's family. His grandmother lived to be 100 and his father, close to 80, recently got married and took a trip to Scotland for the world lawn bowling championships.

Vital Statistics

Pat Cunneen, 52
Date of Birth: September 14, 1933
Born: San Francisco, California
Height: 5'9" **Weight**: 150
Job: Fireman
Lives in: Daly City, California
Activities: Running, swimming, cycling, basketball

I'm running across a lot of old surfing friends who are still in great shape. Maybe it's once having been a surfer, you know, healthy at the beach... once you've tasted that, it's hard to let it go.

I think innately there's some desire, be it freedom or animal-like pleasures that are there, that are cheap. The freedom of surfing, as opposed to the grunting and groaning and the laps and the pushups of a football player. Surfing itself is such a joy.

I had a dog, Polo, and I tried to pattern my life somewhat after him. But with the moral restraints added. He passed on. But we ran together for years. On the beach and the golf course, which in the evening is a primal forest. My dog lived like an animal, probably the best way you can live. I'm a great believer in running and jumping and playing, the way dogs play. Humans ought to do more of that.

Not get too overburdened...

Right. Though you do need a race. You need somebody, whether he's 70 years old or 20, if he's right behind you and you want to beat him or you're right behind him. Be it running, swimming, jumping or playing. A race now and then is real important.

When did you get into cycling?

I've always had a bike. I had a 10-speed when people didn't know what they were, and I always rode it, but just for pleasure. Then I met some fellas at the club that rode a little farther and got into touring. And I enjoy it immensely.

I saw your name in a triathlon magazine as placing in an age group. Did you just start that in the last few years?

As soon as it surfaced, it seemed like a natural thing. It brought together a lot of people from different sports and was fun. It lasts longer. Runs, other than marathons, which I shy away from, are over too soon. Whereas triathlons last for a long time.

How many triathlons did you do last year?

I did the Fireman and then the Iron Horse in Berkeley and the Tin Man Triathlon. I'll do 'em every two weeks, if I'm off.

Did you join the Fire Department right out of high school?

Oh, no. A friend and I got one-way tickets to Hawaii. We were heading to China. But we never got any farther than Hawaii, because we both ended up meeting our wives there. It wasn't such a cheap trip after all. *(Laughter)*

How much do you run a week?

I just try to perspire at least every other day doin' something. Running is number one. I find I can get the best workout from running in the least amount of time and I get the most pleasure from it.

When you swim in the bay, do you run on the beach first to get warm?

No. We have a sauna at the club and I always sit in it before. It's like jogging a slow mile before you go in. I break a sweat.

Doesn't it kill you when you get in?

In the summer the temperature is close to 60°, and that's not too bad. It's after 35 minutes where people

When I started running and lost weight, my mother thought I looked terrible. "Eat more meat and potatoes," she said.

under 150 lbs. start to hurt. Most of your bay swimmers are a little more bulbous on the whole. In winter you just don't stay in as long; it hurts a little more. There's a temperature variation of about 10°. But I still enjoy it.

Do you wear a hat?

Many of us wear wetsuit hats but one of the important things is to keep the hat down at eyebrow level. Many surfing hats come up too high. Another thing that's just as important, if not more so, is ear protection. Keep the water out of the inner ear. I use lambswool and that works like a dream because you don't know it's there. It's not irritating. I wear two bathing caps. Occasionally in the winter I wear a diving cap.

Were you overweight when you decided to give up drinking?

About 15 lbs. But you know, everyone thought I looked better when I was juicing heavily. I had a full face and rosy cheeks. In fact, when I started running and lost weight, my mother thought I looked terrible. "Eat more meat and potatoes," she said.

I thank God that I missed the drug culture. I'm afraid that if someone had said, "Here, one of these red pills makes you feel good," I'd go, "Gimme five." But when we grew up I didn't know anybody that even smoked pot, let alone took downers or uppers or quaaludes. Dope just wasn't for me. I liked the clinking of the ice cubes. I liked getting there slowly. I even enjoyed the hangovers.

Logan Franklin

Pat Cunneen and son Garrett on backpack trip to high Sierras in 1982

(Laughter) Maybe because I'm Irish. The Irish penance the next morning. The little hair of the dog. I enjoyed drinking but it just got the best of me.

So you quit drinking and smoking and started running?

Right. It's the same old story as a lot of people. I started to run to tire the fury and bring out the animal in me. I quit smoking two packs of Camels a day at the same time. My *modus operandi* had always been an unlit cigarette behind my ear. I couldn't get up in the middle of the night to go to the john without firing up.

So what caused you to change?

It was operation bootstrap. I was heading for disaster. I had tried many times to turn my life around and it didn't work. But I had a spiritual effort behind it this time. I returned to my roots. To Christianity. I said, "Hey, I need a little help."

You got back into going to church?

Somewhat. I tried. I still do. But it was the combination of everything. Running really helped. Running is number one. But I thoroughly enjoy cycling or playing a little basketball with the boys or swimming. Swimming—bay swimming, that is—is very similar to long distance running. You can click it off out there and there's a tremendous enjoyment about just being alone in the sea. □

George Farnsworth

Jerry Herlick

I was goin' for 18–20 eggs a week. And rich milk. Bacon and ham. Hash brown potatoes.

Seals and sea lions aren't the only mammals that swim in San Francisco Bay. Year-round, in waters that range from the mid-40s to 60 degrees, a hardy group of swimmers not only defy hypothermia regularly, but swear by the benefits of cold-water swimming. George Farnsworth is one of the most remarkable of these people, not only because of his outstanding swimming ability, but because he had triple by-pass surgery in 1983 and is still swimming 1½ miles a day, 5 days a week. On New Year's Day in 1985 he made his 54th crossing from Alcatraz to San Francisco, a distance of 1-1/16th miles, in 47° water.

Before his heart attack George was swimming 750 miles a year; now he has cut down to 350. Most days he swims with his friend Tom Rice, a Hall-of-Fame football player from the University of San Francisco, later known as the "Masked Marvel", a professional wrestler. They have been swimming together daily for 18 years. Tom, who has injuries from his athletic career, wears fins and hand paddles, so George gets a good workout keeping up with him. "I work my ass off."

George wanted to swim from early on. "I didn't know shit from tar but I just loved the water. When I was five I'd sneak out and go down to the bay, crawlin' on the mud trying to swim." He is, um... colorful. Talking in what sounds like Brooklynese, but is actually Mission District San Francisco working class, in a rich penetrating baritone that carries three blocks, George continually trades taunts, jibes and insults with his swimming pals that would curl a longshoreman's toes. "Hey Al, better go home, the water's too cold for a jackass like you." Or, "Hey look, George got a new swimming cap, looks just like a condom." "You sayin' I look like a prick?" And etc.

Vital Statistics

George Farnsworth, 68
Date of Birth: June 27, 1917
Born: San Francisco, California
Height: 5'9" **Weight:** 170
Job: Retired
Lives in: San Francisco, California
Activities: Swimming, walking

What led up to the heart attack?

I was in a race when it happened, a 2½ mile swim. I was swimmin' good, but after a while, guys that have never beat me were passin' me. I said, "There's something wrong. I guess this is not my day." Then about 200 yards from shore, I started my regular sprint. But there was no sprint in me. I was just going through the motions. Right after that I got the pain. Never directly in the heart. Never that hyperventilation. I just couldn't get the last part of the breath. Then the pain—in the stomach, neck, in my gums. I didn't think it was a heart attack. When I come in I was dizzy, nauseous. But no pain directly in the heart. So I come up to the shower. I was quiet. And the guys said, "Aw, look at Farnsworth. He had a bad swim. He's a sorehead." Ribbin' me. And I said, "Naw, there's something wrong. I don't feel good." I wanted to go home. Be alone. Finally, someone said, "There's something wrong with Farnsworth." So there was a fireman there. He said, "George, don't take a sauna. Take a lukewarm shower." I said, "Now, listen. Don't call a doctor, whatever you do. I'll be all right." But he called the Fire Dept. When they came, soon as shit they called the ambulance right away. Intravenous. Pills. Nitro. Put me on the stretcher. And that was it. St. Francis Hospital. I'd had a heart attack.

So you had a triple?

A triple bi, yeah. I got a little scar. Tip of the heart. Anytime you have a cardiac arrest you have a scar.

They by-pass some of the arteries?

That's right. I had one bad one, in the back. There's the main aorta and the one behind. They had to lift the heart right out. That's over though. It come out good.

How old were you then?

Let me see, I've only had one birthday. I was 66. I'm 67 now. I lied about my age. *(Laughter)* Not that I'm vain, but you know how these guys... they wanted me to go back to the hospital afterwards and do their therapy, you know. Not to make fun, but these old guys do squats and jumping jacks. You'd be there 20 years. I did my own therapy with the help of Tom Rice. With patience and diligence, motivation. You know, I couldn't even walk at first. I felt sorry for myself for the first 2 days. I said, "Shit, no more social life. No more intercourse. No more of this. I'm done." But, you can't do it that way, you gotta fight.

If they let you wear a wetsuit, then you'll want fins and paddles. Next you gotta put a propeller on your ass.

And I'm satisfied now. (Knock on wood.) I may drop dead tomorrow but I feel good.

Did you change your diet any?

Oh, yeah. I was goin' for 18-20 eggs a week. And rich milk. Bacon and ham. Hashed browned potatoes. My mother used to tell me—probably your mother too (in the old days, we didn't know too much about cholesterol)—"You work hard, George. Eat a couple more eggs. They'll stick to your ribs." A lot of bread and butter and bacon. That theory went out the window now.

What do you eat now?

I eat veal, a lot of beans, fish. Quite a bit of fish. And turkey and chicken, no skin. No salt. No more butter. No more hot dogs. No more cold cuts. I haven't had an egg . . . But you see, I'd have ham and eggs and cheese, all that stuff, and I'd work out a little harder. Instead of 2 miles, I'd do 2½. But you can't do that. It's like takin' heroin and cocaine. I was punishing my body and then I'd try and work it off. But it doesn't work that way.

You can burn off the calories but you can't burn off the fat.

That's right. I was damaging the body. The body didn't know what the hell to work off.

Do you cook mostly for yourself?

Yeah. And I go to restaurants where people know me. You can't go in a strange restaurant and order like I do. What the hell, they're too busy. They know that I eat brown bread with every occasion. I'm not a nutritionist but I know enough. I know your flesh-forming foods, your anti-disease factors, protective foods, energy-producing foods. I read a lot since I was in the hospital. It means whether I live 10 or 20 years longer or not.

So you feel good swimming?

This year I'm going to go a little faster. I could've went faster last year. The acid test was the Alcatraz Race on New Year's Day, when the water was 47°. I didn't know how I was going to react. When we jumped off the barge, I waited 4 or 5 minutes. Then I started to go but I never did open up. I didn't know what the cold would do. The doctors were against me. They said cold constricts. But I swam from Alcatraz to the mainland (1-1/16 miles) in 46½ minutes. That's slow for me, but I finished strong. They had a picture in the paper of me comin' in, I was smilin'. And you can't fake a smile. When hypothermia sets in, you're not smilin'.

How do you know if you're getting hypothermia?

That's the funny part. I've had so much experience—I wanna think I'm a little unusual—I can tell. The first clue is all your extremities. Your toes, your head, your fingertips feel a little chilly. Then your stroke . . . You're not relaxing anymore. You think you're going in easy and you're reaching out, but you're not. But the real clue is after an hour, a little more than an hour at 47-50°, you start to feel comfortable. Then you feel warm. That's a bad sign. Then it's like freezin' in the snow. You don't feel any pain. You get a funny smile and you start to hallucinate a little. You see different colors. You know you're in a race but you say, "What am I doin' out here?" But by that time, you won't get out. Once my pilot ordered me out. I thought I was doin' good, but, shit, I was 2 miles off my course. See, I was on my way to hypothermia, which isn't healthy. A lot of people say it don't bother you, but you can do brain damage and organ damage—kidney and liver.

Can you wear a wetsuit?

No, that's considered paraphernalia. You can wear an extra heavy hat. But it doesn't go all the way down the nape of your neck. See, if they let you wear half a wetsuit, then you'll want fins and paddles. Next you gotta put a propeller on your ass. That's part of the swim, the endurance.

Do they figure the tides in these Bay swims?

Oh, yeah, but the tide tables are made a year ahead of time. You have a big rain season, a lot of snow, and you have the run-off. You got billions of gallons of water coming into the Bay. And you only got so much slack. If you're swimmin' at the top of a flood which is high tide, and then she goes into slack and then changes, all that water goes out the Gate. Well, you go as fast as you can just before she hits the top of the flood and you hope you get as far as you can. But if you're out in the middle when she changes, you're not going anywhere. Mark Spitz, you're goin' right out the Gate.

Don Melandry

Are you working now?

No, I was very lucky. I retired just before I was 40. I was in the bar business. Started up a little bar, a nightclub, with dancing. Good, nice, clean. I made a lot of money all at once. But I was a hustler. When I worked, I worked. Put a lot of hours in. Watched the bartender close. During the '50s we were the hottest spot in town. Had a raised bandstand, formica top, felt drapes. I threw all my money in. Took a chance. I wasn't married. Didn't do good right away but then it really went. I mean, I'm not exactly loaded. All I do is eat, swim, fuck and sleep—not always in the same sequence. *(Laughter)* My sex life come back better now since the operation. My glands and all that have been functioning real well. You know, they asked me in an interview, they said, "What do you do for your social life, George?" I say, "Oh, I read a good book. I like legitimate theater. I like to catch an opera now and then." But actually *(Laughter)* it's all bullshit. I'd rather go see *Behind the Green Door.* I'm giving it straight to you, but you gotta tell 'em something, huh? □

George Farnsworth finishing the one-mile swim around Santa Cruz (California) pier in 1979 at age 62. He won first place in his age division.

Joan Flint

Lloyd Kahn, Jr.

Every June a unique show takes place at a small theater in Berkeley, California. It's called Tap Dance Extravaganza *and over the years it's become a community affair. Over 100 dancers participate. Not just dancing, but making costumes, doing the sets, handling the lights and music. The performance is the showcase for dancers from the Tappin' Fancy studio of Oakland and the brainchild of Joan Flint. Joan started the studio in 1976 after living several years on the coast above Mendocino.*

Vital Statistics
Joan Flint, 52
Date of Birth: February 10, 1933
Born: Worcester, Massachusetts
Height: 5'5" **Weight**: 115
Job: Dance instructor, choreographer
Lives in: Oakland, California
Activities: Dancing, aerobic classes

What were you doing in the late '60s?

My ex-husband and I started an alternative school up the coast near Mendocino.

What kind of kids? Hippies?

Oh, everybody was a hippy then. *(Laughter)* Even the rednecks were hippies. They were kids who were mostly fed up with drugs and wanted to be back in nature, grow their own food, that kind of thing. A younger version of the Haight Ashbury.

What about the 3 R's?

We felt the academics were equally as important as the arts, so we had physics and English literature as well as lots of crafts, a vegetable garden, raising animals, milking the cows. It was 70 acres and everybody lived there.

It's amazing to look back at those years, isn't it?

Yeah. You know, about 2 months ago, we were driving around the Berkeley campus and suddenly there were these people in tie-dyed skirts with backpacks and little kids and dogs and psychedelic stuff all over them. We had just gone through fraternity row with all the preppies and their short haircuts. And here is this incredible flashback! "What is going on here? Where did these people come from?" Well, it was a Grateful Dead concert. And all the Dead freaks had come out of the woodwork.

What do you think about all that happened?

I think there was a real camaraderie between people, a real joy. That's what I saw. There were drugs, but you know, kids go through something; if it's not drugs it's something else. And when did men start wearing bright clothes? It wasn't until the Beatles stepped out in a cape or two.

How did you start tap dancing?

I started a class with maybe 5 kids who were kinda nuts about it. When the school broke up and I moved to Berkeley, I thought, "What do I really want to do? I really want to

It's like playing drums with your feet.

Joan in a sequence from a solo number in her dance studio's annual Tap Dance Extravaganza

dance." And tap dancing had been kind of dormant from the late '50s on. The only people tap dancing were the old black guys. It never died in soul but it certainly died in popularity. So when I decided to start doing it again, it was not a popular time for it. But I took over this studio anyway and started doing classes and more and more people came.

Is it good exercise?

Tap is real aerobic . . . plus it's such fun. I mean, it's a skill. It's like playing drums with your feet. It's a terribly exciting form of dance.

Where did it come from?

It came from Africa first. It was also a combination of the Irish clogging and what the blacks were doing in the South when they started fooling around in the 1800s.

Is it hard to learn?

A lot of people have the feeling that it's easy, because they've seen the Hollywood movies. But it's not. It requires a lot of coordination and concentration. Some people don't come with that and really have to work hard to get it. Most people can get it if they persevere. It just takes some people a little longer.

Do you need to be loose?

Most people are not loose. That's not one of the requirements, but if you can relax into it, getting loose just happens. It definitely helps to be loose because most of the movement is from the knees on down. We do a lot of ankle exercises and warm-ups. But see, it's hard to hurt yourself tap dancing.

That's great. Like cross-country skiing, maybe it's just a complete exercise in itself.

The only people who have problems are people who have started with a problem—like a spur on the heel or a knee problem. But I can't remember anyone hurting themselves

When the school broke up and I moved to Berkeley, I thought, "What do I really want to do? I really want to dance."

tap dancing. It's the kind of thing where you're using everything in a fairly balanced way.

How old are your students?

We have ages 6 to 65. A lot of people come in who've wanted to do it for years. They've watched a lot of Fred Astaire or Gene Kelly. Often their first question is, "Am I too old for this? I'm 30 or 40." Or, "Are there any men in the class?"

Are there?

More and more men, but they're very surprised when they come in and try to keep up with the women.

Tell me about Tap Dance Extravaganza.

Oh, it's fantastic. It brings together all these people who are dentists, teachers, construction workers . . . everything. It's an incredible show, it's not a recital. It's like a Busby Berkeley musical–lots of people. We have sewing workshops so the costumes are out of sight! I think we're going to sell out all five nights this time. I really do. □

Diane Gilkerson

Joan Flint and Craig Barnes in their Fred and Ginger number

Jack Fulton

Lloyd Kahn, Jr.

Jack Fulton is a native Californian, a photographer, part-time carpenter and, in the past few years, runner and cyclist. He got into running and cycling a little at a time, found himself doing more as time went by and now runs 4-6 miles several times a week and takes occasional mountain bike camping trips in the Southwest with his long-time friend and neighbor Rodger Jacobsen. Along the way Jack has lost 10 pounds.

I've known Jack since the early '60s. When I got into publishing I'd contact him whenever there was any kind of photo assignment.

I don't know how the art critics describe his photos, but a few things about his approach to photography always struck me. First, he didn't carry around the usual arsenal of camera bodies, lenses, light meters, metal suitcases. It was one camera, one lens, that was it. Secondly, his photos, and this became more apparent as he transitioned from black and white into color, were beautifully composed, like paintings. He'd go to great lengths to get in the right position, sprawled on his stomach underneath a barbed wire fence, balanced precariously on a fence post.

Jack has exhibited in galleries throughout the country and had just returned from a photo assignment in Paris when we did this interview. He's also a teacher and chairman of the photography department at the San Francisco Art Institute.

Vital Statistics

Jack Fulton, 46
Date of Birth: June 30, 1939
Born: San Francisco, California
Height: 5'10½" **Weight**: 180
Job: Photographer, builder
Lives in: San Rafael, California
Activities: Running, cycling

I've been showing people these interviews, and everybody seems to like the idea.

If you're at all halfway fit you feel wonderfully happy when somebody else recognizes it in a humorous way. 'Cause life is a delight, you know, and this physical stuff is wonderful.

What got you into bike riding?

About 15 years ago, I went to a police auction and bought a bike made out of a bunch of parts. And I just rode it around now and then.

Have you gone bike camping?

To Horseshoe Canyon, to the Maze, in Utah. And then another one around the Ruby Mountains in Nevada. And then we took one through the White Rim Trail in Utah.

What does the mountain bike do for you?

The bike allows you to cover a huge amount of territory in a very primitive area. Many of the areas we go into are accessible only to four-wheel-drive vehicles.

Couldn't you just go on hiking trails?

Technically, you're not supposed to. You just shouldn't do it. It ruins trails.

On your last trip, how long were you away from your car?

We go about 35 miles a day. So we go about 3 to 4 days away from the car.

With how much water apiece?

About five gallons.

You don't run across any water?

We always plan it so we'll encounter a spring or a river about two-thirds of the way through. You wanna always make sure when you're out in the desert that even when you get to water you'll have pretty close to a gallon left.

Did you swim on the White Rim Trail trip?

The water's pretty cold. And last time it was flooded. We had to walk 5 miles through a flooded river with the bikes on our shoulders. Then you put it on the road and go a quarter of a mile and then you're back in the water again. If you swam in those floods, you'd disappear.

What did you guys take for food?

In the desert we took canned food 'cause it has water in it. If you take dried food, you have to carry the water to put into the food.

What kind of canned food? Beans?

We took Del Monte Mexican Style Tomatoes and beans with hot stuff in it and tortillas. A little bit of cheese. And we rolled 'em up and made tacos.

How about breakfast?

Uh . . . tacos. *(Laughter)*

Jack Fulton

Three times a day?

No, no, no. We had excellent soups, from packages. We'd have maybe a can of beans. Sometimes we'd take a can of white potatoes. We'd have real good vegetable stews.

So you'd go about 4 days away and then you'd be back to the car.

Yeah. And then we'd drive somewhere else and do another 100 mile trip.

Did you see anybody else on mountain bikes on any of these trips?

No. The first time we went last year . . . yes, we did. When we first went down we ran into two people on mountain bikes but they were too blown out by it. It blew their minds that they even did it and they were leaving. They were exhausted. Last year when we went to the Maze, a couple of people on mountain bikes had been in there before us.

Did you guys lose weight on these trips?

Maybe about 2 lbs. I lost more weight in France that I did on these trips.

How come?

I guess we drink too much. I don't know. The first trip we took some bourbon and vodka. *(Laughter)* One night we were on top of Nine-Mile Canyon, a hundred miles from any place and probably drank a fifth just sittin' there lookin' at the stars in a lightning storm.

What did you go over to Paris for?

I won an award from Paris Audio Visual and the City of Paris to photograph the city.

Is it a big, noisy, frightening city?

No, it's the greatest city I've ever been in my life. Bar none. I must have walked 10 miles a day. You know, in Paris I lost weight because I was really enthralled with life. And I think that's one of the things that sports has given me—not that it's given me a reason to live, but I think for most people, you've gotta have your job and very few people have an opportunity to be singly employed or to direct themselves with their life, and sports is a single direction and also, if you wish, you can compete. So it supports me to have far better health and I think it has made me a

Rodger Jacobsen

Left, Rodger Jacobsen and Jack Fulton at the Maze, Canyonlands, Utah.

Right, Jack on the White Rim Trail on the same trip.

happier person. I think it has made me younger looking; it's made me a more handsome person . . . *(Laughter)*

Sports gives you some kind of reason to not overindulge.

Yeah. I really believe that life is physical and death is mental. Really, I think that when we die and are put in the grave or are cremated or whatever happens, that's the end of your physical state. Life that we lead with our eyeballs and our stomachs and our legs and our body odors and stuff, that's physical. The exercise of my physical self has been, *ever* since I was a kid, a joy. As a kid, I'd run and run and run, and hike and hike and hike, and I'm glad I got back to that in my older age. And gram by gram I'm losing weight. I'm not on a crash program. I used to go on diets to try to make myself attractive. I just don't do that now.

How long have you and Rod been friends?

Since 1949. He just lives 2½ miles away.

So you guys have been working out together for a few years now? And you run together and you take these trips together.

Yeah. I think we're rare. I think very few men have intimate friends like that. We can talk about anything we want to one another.

Are you guys competitive?

A tiny bit. But not competitive to the point where we're trying to best one another. Like, for instance, when I came back from Paris the other day, we went running. We'd both run solo along this same route before. Once I'd done it in 52 minutes, and he couldn't even get below 55. The last time I ran it, I did 56:30. So I said, "Gee, Rod . . . if we keep this pace up, we're going to break the record." And we came in at about 51:40 or something. I pulled him up the hills and he pushed me in the flats. It was a real nice exchange. And we broke his record and broke the record that I had set up. □

Jeff Galloway

Dave Stock

Everybody's favorite story about Jeff Galloway took place at the 1972 Olympic trials. Two months before the trials, Jeff, Frank Shorter and Jack Bacheler had gone to Vail, Colorado to train in the high altitude. Then at the trials, Jeff, primarily a marathoner, unexpectedly made the Olympic team in the 10K while Bacheler was disqualified. In the marathon trials the next week, Jeff paced Bacheler, then dropped back at the finish line to let him win and qualify for the Olympic team.

The same spirit has characterized Jeff's 25-year-old running career: he likes to help others, and to teach. In 1973 he founded Phidippides, now a 35-store chain of running stores. In 1975 he opened his first of three fitness vacation camps. He spends a lot of time traveling around the country, giving talks at pre-race dinners, helping race directors and coaching runners of all abilities. He was the winner of the Atlanta Peachtree Road Race in 1970 and later was the key organizer of the event. He was co-founder of the Avon International Women's Marathon in 1978, which lead to the womens's Olympic marathon.

Jeff set an American record in the 10 mile in 1973 (47:49), has a best time of 27:21 in the 10K and ran a 2:16 marathon at age 35. His training theories are widely quoted in the running magazines and he has just published Galloway's Book on Running.

Vital Statistics
Jeff Galloway, 40
Date of Birth: July 12, 1945
Born: Raleigh, North Carolina
Height: 5'10½" **Weight**: 135
Job: Owner, Phidippides International; race advisor; running coach, author
Lives in: Atlanta, Georgia
Activities: Running

Interestingly enough, the running movement seems to have started in 1964. In that year both the Boston Marathon and the Bay to Breakers, which had been erratic in their enrollment, started an upward trend which has continued to the present day.

In general, young people in the '60s were expressing a desire for improvement in their lives. I think their attitudes then were, "I'm not really content with things right now." Or you can look at it from the left brain/right brain viewpoint. A person who operated primarily from the left-brain side, the logical side, tended to get motivated by Cooper's book (*Aerobics*). But many others probably got into it for more right-brain benefits and intuitions—they *sensed* that this was good for them.

Somebody told me recently he thought that you and Shorter and Kenny Moore and Bill Rodgers were a different generation of runners, that people identified with you because you had long hair and were more hip than runners had been.

We really were not motivated by specific goals. And I think that was characteristic of my generation. We were not really interested in the money aspect, because there wasn't any. We were all interested in just doing the best we could. The fact that we had long hair or beards or mustaches was just symbolic in that we looked like other members of our generation.

How did the masses of runners get into racing?

In the early '70s people thought, "Well, I better do this for my health." Then after some momentum built, one or two people in an office started running. Then came the social aspect and fun runs became very popular. These are low-key, non-racing situations in which 2 or more people get together. "I'll meet you at the corner on Saturday morning at 9 o'clock." These informal groups started growing. What started out as 8 or 9 would get to 50 or 60. And it was a natural evolution to organized races. By 1977, running became the thing to do. You saw movie stars running, and lots of ads on television with people running—a lot of fad runners, people who got caught up in the aura and excitement. A lot of people dropped out in the '80s but there were still so many new runners that you never saw a falling off in total numbers. Now, in the mid-80s the running population is much more knowledgeable, much more solid. The runner knows why he wants to run. It's not because somebody else is running or it's the thing to do anymore. He gets something out of it personally.

What do you perceive is happening right now?

Most people are running for the stress reduction. People still have a wide

Dave Stock

range of reasons for being out there—the competition, the heart exercise—but reducing stress is at the top of the list.

Really? It went from health reasons to a fad to stress reduction?

Exactly. Don't get me wrong. Even though it was a fad, it was not a fad like the hula hoop. It was a fad akin to a health diet. Like if we eat bean sprouts we're going to be healthy or something. That's what a lot of people did feel. They were going to be healthy and all these wonderful things would happen to them if they started running. Well, that was naive. Good things *did* happen, but it wasn't a panacea, it didn't make everything in a person's life better.

You find this in talking to runners as you travel around?

Yes. Of course there are still a few who get into it for competition, who want to recreate their days of glory in high school or whatever, after years of inactivity. There are still lots of people who know they need the heart exercise, and a wide range of other reasons. But most people I talk to these days are in it for stress reduction.

What are you doing yourself these days?

Believe it or not, I adhere to my own advice in having easy weeks. I run between 60 and 80 miles one week, then about 30-40 miles the next. I take at least 2 days completely off a week. Sometimes I'll do alternative exercise and other times I won't do anything on those days.

Are you doing any races in the future? *(Jeff had just recovered from a groin injury that persisted for over a year.)*

Wide World Photos

Jeff qualifying in 1972 Olympic 10K trials. Teammate Frank Shorter waits to greet him at left.

Yeah. To train, I am doing regular accelerations twice a week. Not all out. I just run nice and light and bouncy and within myself, but faster than normal. Also, once a week, I run hills to help strengthen the legs.

On August 10, 1985, Jeff and his old running pals, all in their late '30s or early '40s ran in the Run With the Stars 10K *in Oxnard, California. They haven't slowed down much at all:*
Bill Rodgers: 29:09!
Frank Shorter: 30:19
Don Kardong: 31:30
Tracy Smith: 31:53
Jeff Galloway: 32:02
Amby Burfoot: 34:28 □

Most people I talk to these days are in it for stress reduction.

George Clark

Peachtree Road Race in Atlanta, Georgia, 1976. Don Kardong (771), Ed Leddy (878) and Galloway (513). Kardong won, Bill Rodgers was second, Galloway fourth.

Johnnie Hammond

Vital Statistics
Johnnie Hammond, 51
Date of Birth: March 19, 1934
Born: Richmond, California
Height: 5'5" **Weight**: 150
Job: Seamstress, short story writer, grandmother
Lives in: Vallejo, California
Activities: Running, camping, fishing, skating, bowling

Roi Hammond

There's a TV show on in San Francisco on Saturday nights called Hot Streaks. *The show is for kids, and the host is ex-49er wide receiver Gene Washington. One night, Gene interviewed a boxer from Vallejo, California, named Royan (Destroyin' Royan) Hammond. The camera showed Royan, an up and coming middleweight, working out in the gym, sparring, at home with his family and in one sequence, running around the track with a woman who looked like his older sister. What a surprise to hear that this was Royan's mother, Johnnie Hammond.*

Johnnie is 51 years old. She was born in Texas and came to California when her parents were hired to work in the shipyards in Richmond during World War II.

Johnnie has worked as a seamstress in a commercial laundry, and with handicapped children. But after surgery in 1969 to remove one kidney she was placed on permanent disability.

After years of moving around as an Air Force family, the Hammonds settled in Vallejo. Johnnie is divorced but not alone. She is mother to 8 children and grandmother to 13 more. Out in front of her house is her car, with a bumper sticker reading "Foxy Grandma."

Well see, all my children . . . they all got Roy in their names. The oldest boy is Roy. OK, let's start it. Royce (he's the oldest, Royce), Roycelyn; then there's Roy, then there's Roi; then there's Royette, and Royal, Royan and Roycecia—we call her Roycia for short.

Was their father named Roy or something?

Yes. *(Laughter)*

When you'd yell out the door for them to come in from playing, how'd they know who you were calling for?

We have nicknames for them.

When they were growing up dinner time must have been a real circus.

It was like I was cookin' for an army. It was. I had great big pots so when everybody left home I gave all the big pots away.

Tell me about your history of exercising.

In high school I played basketball, softball, soccer, volleyball and badminton. But you know what they didn't have that I wish I would've had? Track for girls. I was in pretty good shape in high school and college at Contra Costa College.

I started having kids when I was about 20, but I stayed in shape. I used to exercise with Jack LaLanne. *(Laughter)* I was smaller than I am, but over the years you know . . . but I used to exercise in front of the TV every morning. Then the kids would get down and exercise . . . the ones that weren't in school.

I felt better doing stuff like that. I also kept playing, you know . . . when the kids were growing up I'd take 'em to the park and play sports with them. And they were all interested in sports. I'd play baseball and go to their games.

When did you start running?

When three of them started boxing. They would get up early in the morning. We couldn't afford sweatsuits, so what they would do was use garbage bags, cut arms in 'em and

wrap it around them. And I would do this too. We'd get up about 6 o'clock and we would run. This was in '72–'73. From then on when they got older . . . well, Roy would come by the house and we would go over to the high school track and run together.

I couldn't keep up with him at first. But then I started making it around the track. I could make it around the track five times then without stopping. I was in really good shape. We'd go over to the track and stay there about 2 hours. We wouldn't just run around the track for 2 hours. We'd run through the streets, and over to the track.

What kind of food do you eat?

I don't eat steak or pork. I'm more of a vegetarian and I make my own menus. I mix vegetables. What I've really started cooking with lately is lettuce and vegetables mixed together. And I don't use salt. I use garlic powder. No dairy products either. I stay away from that. Maybe once a week I might have an egg. I eat lots of cereal. I like oatmeal.

I have fish or chicken three or four times a week. I catch my own fish. We have a pier right over here. We have the bay. And the Sacramento River is good to fish too. I catch a lot of striped bass and perch.

Do you smoke? Drink coffee?

No. I did drink coffee but I quit.

Does the kidney thing slow you down?

It does now that I'm getting older. I feel myself gettin' a little tired. Now what I do is I run and I walk, run and walk. I don't just run straight anymore.

I take 16 pills a day for my kidneys. I had one removed and the other one is bad. It has stones in it but it's still working.

Can it get better with good diet?

Well, every time I get X-rays the stones are still there. But they're not forming, or getting worse. I figured with the diet and the medicine, that's helping.

What do you do these days for exercise?

Now I only run 3 hours a week. I can't do more. But I walk. I do more walking.

Do you do something every day?

Uh-huh. I go over to the community center three days a week. It's a drop-in exercise and recreation program. We have an instructor and we go through thirty minutes of exercise. I've done aerobics but that was a little too much for me to keep up with. So I do that, I go over to the waterfront to run and I do my own exercises. I got this book from *Reader's Digest: Eat Better–Live Better*—I'm always reading—and it has exercises in there to do. I have a little portable exerciser that I pull out and lay on the floor. It has the little bicycle things that go around and I use that when it's raining.

I'll never quit exercising completely. Once you get started, you have more energy and just feel better about yourself. □

Roi Hammond

Above left: Johnnie, right, with her sister Audrey (middle) and a friend at Contra Costa College, Richmond, California, 1952. Above right: Johnnie with her oldest son Royce and grandchildren Dontay, 10, and Royce, Jr., 8 in 1985.

Michael Jeneid

Michael Jeneid seems to have compressed the activities and adventures of three lives into one. He is or has been a runner, pentathlete, steeplechase jockey, cross-country ski racer, kayaker, Royal Marine, mountain climber and survivalist as well as a Shakespearean scholar, author, lecturer, bird-watcher and artist. He has written books on cross-country skiing, Nordic ski training and is just completing a book called Shakespeare's Birds of Prey *(illustrated with his own watercolors). Michael now lives in Stinson Beach, California, in a small house where he can watch the birds on the Bolinas Lagoon from his studio window.*

I used to hold the record for making it from England to France by kayak. It took 4 hours and 53 minutes. I also kayaked from London to Paris once. It took me 6 weeks. I started right in the middle of London, down the Thames, along the coast to Dover, over to France and all the way around the coast.

I did it because I was totally broke and had an appointment with a girl in Paris that summer. So I bought my kayak with 5 pounds down, packed up 15 pounds worth of equipment and food and off I went. And, boy, I starved. And I got very cold. But I got there. And it became a national story. It was in all the newspapers. The girl I was meeting was a debutante and a beautiful girl, so they put it in all the gossip columns.

Vital Statistics

Michael Jeneid, 52
Date of Birth: September 18, 1933
Born: London, England
Height: 5'11" **Weight**: 152
Job: Nordic ski school director, writer, painter
Lives in: Stinson Beach, California/Lake Tahoe, California
Activities: Running, cross country skiing, kayaking

Did you grow up in London?

Well, I was born in London, but I left London at age 6 because they were busy bombing it. I went to a prep school. From there to a public school. And from there into the Royal Marines. When I enlisted in the Royal Marines I was 18½ and weighed 140 lbs. And I was 5'10". That's pretty light. It quickly became apparent that I was a good runner—as they rushed us around from point A to point B, I was always the first person there. When I was 25, at the Royal Naval College in Greenwich, we had the annual athletic thing, and I won the half-mile, the mile and the 3 miles all in the same competition.

Seven years later in Australia, when I was a captain in the Australian Infantry Corps, I entered the Australian Army Championships and I won the half-mile, mile and 3 miles again. Seven years later in exactly the same way. I was 32 years old. I won the half in 1:58. I won the mile in 4:26. And I won the 3 miles in 14:58. I served in the Royal Marines for 7 years and I competed in the modern pentathlon. In 1958, I put up the world's best mark for 3 of those events—cross-country horse riding, fencing and running.

John Echols

After I resigned from the Royal Marines, I was a civilian for a year and wrote a book, which wasn't published. Then I enlisted in the paratroopers because I'd heard that the paratroopers were starting a modern pentathlon team. I stayed with the paratroopers 5 years . . . But they'll only let you do that for so long. So I had to go back to soldiering. I became an instructor in the British Army Outward Bound School, which I really loved.

So what do you do in Outward Bound in England?

Outward Bound as the British started it is quite straightforwardly character development through arduous training. It's as simple as that. Americans shy away from that, you know. They don't like talking about character training. Americans are supposed to do what they want to do. The British thing is very rigorous, indeed. It involves kayaking, cross-country running, living out in the cold and the wet and working together as a team.

Here's what you'd do with a kid in Outward Bound school in England. You'd say, "Hey, c'mon. You're 18 years old. You're behaving like a shithead. You're going to have a miserable life if you keep this up. So, let's change the direction and start having a good one." The purpose is to make you a stronger person as a result of very intensive group activities where you have to accept leadership roles or following

We once sailed an open whale boat from Hurricane Island, Maine, down to Manhattan. It was a very, very cold journey. November.

John Echols

Michael Jeneid on roller skis, used for cross-country ski training in off-season

roles. It doesn't matter which. It depends on what sort of person you are. You give each person his chance to lead—but if he's no good at it, you don't leave him in that position. You say, "OK, be a good follower." In this country, for instance, the only place you see proper leadership and proper organization is in the business world. The Sierra Club—a bunch of hush puppies. Thousands of committees all covering each others asses.

How long have you been in this country?

Sixteen years now. The most useful thing I've done here, I think, was working in New York City as a drug addiction specialist for Phoenix House. I took them rock climbing, kayaking. We once sailed an open whale boat from Hurricane Island, Maine, down to Manhattan. It was a very, very cold journey. November. Below freezing for 12 days straight. After that trip I was taken extremely ill and very nearly died. I got phlebitis in both legs.

How did the guys do?

Fantastic. All the training I'd had as a commando soldier, I was able to apply directly to these guys. They loved it! My students were coming out of that experience so goddamn strong they were saying things like, "Fuck Phoenix House. I don't need Phoenix House." And they were right. Phoenix House would hit you about the head and say, "Dummy! You can't do it on your own. Do it our way." The guy comes and takes a course with me and I treat him like a real decent human being. By golly, he's got to work hard. He's gotta do right. But I never swear at him. I never tell him he's an asshole. I tell him, "You can only go up from here." They come out of this experience saying, "Hey, I'm not such a bad shit after all."

To bring it up to date now, what is it you've been doing this year?

This year I spent my whole summer finishing my Shakespeare book. Working on my house that I bought in Stinson Beach. And trying to decide whether to ski professionally this winter or just ski for myself. I'm not wealthy, you know. But I'm never in debt either. I earn my living from whatever I'm doing. Whatever skills I have I market. One of my primary skills is teaching skiing, so right now I'm working fulltime as the director of skiing for the Sierra Club at their lodge in Norden.

I'm also writing a book called *Difficult Journeys*. It's about survival and I'm very deliberately challenging the concept of survival that's being put out every day by magazines like *Outside* where people go and challenge very difficult projects. Which is fine, I'm not knocking that. But I'm saying that most of the time on those journeys, if you want to back off you can. In fact, most people do. The examples I've used are a night ambush in a battle where either you or the other guy is going to die tonight. I've used escaping from a prison. I've picked 3 incidents that are not out there on your personal adventure or fun expedition. What I'm after is not how many bullets you fired or how brave you are. What I'm after is what do you do about the problem. That you're about to be killed if you don't get it right. The third one I used is my convict trip and the boat. You see, we got into terrible trouble. Extremely rough water. □

Connie Johnstone

Jack Fulton

R.C. Young

Connie Johnstone doesn't run in races, doesn't read running magazines and isn't sure what model running shoe she wears. Yet every morning at 5:30, summer or winter, rain or shine, she slips out of bed and runs for an hour before going to work. She's been doing this now for over 16 years and—competitive runners, take note—has never had a running injury.

I started running shortly after having my fourth child. This was in 1968. I had a vein stripping job on my legs, and after the operation I thought, "Here I am, 30 years old and I've got four kids and a whole bunch of physical things that just aren't right." I was kind of limping along after the operation and I thought . . . this is it. Running is cheap. I can do it if I get up early enough before the kids are out of bed. I'll try it. I don't want to be a nice fat lady with four children.

So I started running with a friend in the morning. I would brag, "I ran all the way to the community center," which was about a half mile away. I thought that was wonderful. I'd only been at it about a month and I was bragging around the neighborhood. Another gal said, "I can do that." She wasn't impressed at all. And she smoked a lot—2 or 3 packs a day. I smoked too, but less than a pack a day. We raced, and she beat me. We did that for a long time. We'd go out long before anybody got up when it was still dark. I like to run alone now. I don't really need to go with anyone.

Vital Statistics
Connie Johnstone, 45
Date of Birth: December 28, 1940
Born: Philadelphia, Pennsylvania
Height: 5'9½" **Weight**: 135
Job: Publications manager
Lives in: San Rafael, California
Activities: Running

Did you quit smoking?

Not right away. Smoking had a hold on me. One day I called a friend of mine and said, "How you doing, Angelo?" He said, "I'm curled up in a corner in fetal position." I asked what was the matter and he said, "I haven't had a cigarette in 48 hours." "I'll help you out, Angelo," I told him. "I'll bet you $200. The first person to smoke has to pay the other guy $200." He said, "I can't do it. I'm in agony." I prodded him but he refused. I told my boss at work about trying to get Angelo to bet and he said that he would bet with me instead. The boss was 45 years old. Big, handsome guy. "It's a matter of life or death with me," he said. "I must quit smoking."

So I said OK. I went around the office and told everyone about the bet. Within 4 days he was back smoking. He told me he had a stressful weekend coming up and needed to smoke. "I'll bet you after this weekend," he said. So we started again. He lasted 24 hours. The end of that month, he had a massive stroke.

Did he die?

No, but now he drags his leg slightly. Boy . . . I never smoked another cigarette after that.

You consider yourself a jogger?

Absolutely not. A runner.

What effect has running had on your life?

The physical benefits are that you have a better body, you're more attractive. There's no doubt about that. Whatever you've got, you've maximized it. I won't tell you, but I could tell you some interesting stories about what effect it's had on my life. But that's the X-rated interview.

C'mon tell me.

No way. *(Laughter)* Just let me say that it has totally changed my life. It's truly amazing.

Running has made me much more of an individual and not just a mother. A lot of people over 40 get into becoming just mothers. I mean what else are you going to do?

Running also helps me overcome fear. Like when I got divorced, I was left with four children under 15. During that time I'd be out running and I'd be crying. But it's always better to run and cry than not to run at all. If you're running, you're not going crazy. You aren't drinking too much. You're still doing the healthy thing. It's very reassuring. Any time my life takes a turn for the worse—I have a very smooth life really—but when something traumatic happens I increase the running. If I were to give up running at a difficult time in my life, I'd be afraid for myself. As long as I'm running, I'm not so scared.

What do your kids think about your running?

My kids have a very different attitude about me than other mothers. They respect the athletic part. My daughter, who's 24, told me not long ago that it used to make her jealous that I had the will to get up every day and go out. She said, "You know how you

It's always better to run and cry than not to run at all. If you're running, you're not going crazy.

used to come in and say, 'Did 5 good miles today.' I used to open the bathroom, go in and slam the door. I did not want to hear that." She said, "My mother is out running 5 miles a day and I'm doing nothing." That was the attitude. Mom is not supposed to be doing anything that you can't do, right? Except maybe bake a pie or something. It gives you a little different perspective on your mama.

Have you ever thought of racing?

People try to get me to race, but I know I'd be terrible. So I don't compete. I figure I should just try to be as natural about it as I can. What I can do fairly easily, I do. That's the way I am.

What do you think your parents' generation is missing out on by not being physically active?

Being young for about 20 more years. I mean that sincerely; young physically and mentally.

Do you ever get "runner's high"?

I have. It actually made me cry. That feeling! I run in the most beautiful place. I'd been running and running and running one morning, slow jog you know, and I got up to the top of the hill and I looked out and I don't know why but I kept saying, "My eyes, my eyes." I just *saw* this beauty. I felt grateful for sight and for being able to run. Just moving is a wonderful thing. I got a tremendous rush of gratitude to God Almighty for letting me be. I *am*. It was just great. □

Jack Fulton

Connie Johnstone out on her daily pre-dawn run

Don Kahn

Don Kahn was a friend of mine in high school (Lowell High, San Francisco, class of 1952). Don married his high school sweetheart, Rosalyn Schwartz, in 1954 and they now have three children, ages 28, 27 and 23 . . . and a new grandson.

Last time I saw Don, I noticed he ordered a salad for lunch, with no dressing and wasn't putting any butter on his bread. Pretty unusual. It turned out he'd recently had a cholesterol scare and spent two weeks at the Pritikin Research Foundation Center in Santa Monica, California. He'd given up coffee, most hard liquor, fatty foods and started to exercise. He'd cut his cholesterol from 320 to 170, lost about 20 pounds and had no doubts that the Pritikin experience had enhanced the quality as well as prolonged the duration of his life.

Don and Roz Kahn

People had always been telling me you've got to lose 25 lbs., you've got to exercise, you have to diet, quit smoking, all of that. But I always felt OK. I could always play tennis and Roz and I were a good doubles team. And I knew, I wasn't stupid, that drinking wasn't good for you. I knew that smoking wasn't good for you so I was lying all the time. I would tell people I didn't smoke. Wouldn't buy any and then bum cigarettes. I must have been smoking at least a pack a day. But if you'd have asked me then I would've told you a couple of cigarettes. Then my dad passed away in February of '83 and I went to Pritikin's.

What was it like?

You stay in the old Santa Monica Country Club. It's not fancy—they don't want it to be. They want you to know you're working. It's not furnished nicely. It's not a spa. It's south of Malibu on the beach. A real old 1920s kind of place.

The first day you go there, you have a complete medical. The best medical checkup as far as cardiograms and cholesterol tests and all those kinds of things that I ever had. Then there's the head trip in which they talk to you about stress, diet, exercise. They have cooking classes. They literally show you movies or slides of what happens when you eat cheese, what is going on in your system. They tell you no oils, not because they think it's bad for your heart but they've noticed since people have been using polyunsaturated oils there's a lot of cancer. Therefore, they teach you how to get by without any oil.

What happened when you came out of there 2 weeks later? What was your weight?

After 2 weeks, I'd lost about 14 lbs. I really quit smoking for the first time. I had learned to race-walk. So

Vital Statistics

Don Kahn, 51
Date of Birth: February 5, 1935
Born: San Francisco, California
Height: 5'11" **Weight:** 181
Job: General business
Lives in: San Francisco, California
Activities: Walking, swimming, weight lifting

After 4 or 5 days of Pritikin, my energy level was soaring. I don't know if it was the smoking, the caffeine. . . But I'm telling you, my energy!

I've been aerobically exercising half an hour every day since. It gave me the impetus—once you see why, then you do it. I had given up alcohol; I've gone back to it but in a very minimal way. In fact, I would say that 99% of my alcohol today is beer because I know that carbohydrates are going through me quickly.

What's your cholesterol now?

About 170. And it was 170 when I left. My triglycerides, which was another thing they measured there, were in half. When I was there, I think I was one of the 5 healthiest people. A lot of people had had by-pass surgery. In fact, Rock Hudson had been there, he's had a triple by-pass. His doctor had told him that he would have to get another one and a way to avoid it was to quit smoking and give up these fatty foods. He was there 4 days and walked out. He preferred the miracle of surgery. I don't. I'm scared to death of that stuff.

A lot of times there's friction in the family if one person gets into something like that, but you two seem to have done it together.

Well, Roz and I are still very much in love and she wants me to live. Let me tell you, if there was any friction, it was mine in not wanting to reform, but her insisting that we live a long healthy life. There is today a tiny bit of friction in that we're back on a schedule where we go out a lot. And when we're going out, I say, "God, I shouldn't be going out. I can't keep up with my diet." And she says, "You know better than that. You can order properly."

What do you eat when you go out?

Pasta without dressing and salad without dressing. Or fish. But in reality, Pritikin is not real big on fish or chicken either. I lost 14 lbs. at the center. I came out of there, I lost another 11. In the last 4 months, and particularly since working out on the Nautilus, I've put back 8 of the total of 25. And of that 8, I think 2 of it should have come back and 6 of it is just bullshit.

The most important thing that I could tell anyone about Pritikin is . . . Roz and I went to Hawaii . . . and I knew something was basically wrong. I didn't have a 2 martini lunch every day, but the 2 times a week I did was easily going to become the 3. I was smoking more. I was drinking more coffee. I was nervous and extremely tired. And that's not my style. We'd get up in the morning, go down to the beach. I'd swim, but easily. I'd come back, lay in the sun and fall asleep. Three o'clock, everybody would say let's get up, go shower and have a drink. I'd lay down and fall asleep. I was beat. I swear to God, after 4 or 5 days of Pritikin, at 5 o'clock at night Roz would say what do you want to do and I'd say let's go for a walk. My energy level was just soaring. I don't know if it was the smoking; I don't know if it was the caffeine. The first 2 days of Pritikin when you give up caffeine, I couldn't get my head up off the bed. But I knew it was important to quit the smoking. I'm telling you, my energy! The chief exercise there is these machines that resemble a cardiogram/treadmill test. I swear a couple times I felt I was going to burst right through the god-damn wall, I felt so powerful. At my best days in athletics, I don't think that I felt as strong as that. That was clearly either the not smoking, the not drinking or the diet.

Pritikin's diet standard is that you don't eat 3 meals, you eat all the time. Smaller portions all day long. I think it's a matter of timing. Here's a typical day's meal at Pritikin. Now remember the portions are small. First thing in the morning you have cooked cereal with no milk or half a glass of nonfat milk. Never skimmed milk, always nonfat. Half a banana. And a piece of natural wheat toast. Pritikin, incidentally, does not use toasters because he believes that anything burnt is carcinogenic. So it's like dried toast in an oven. Maybe apple butter on the toast. About an hour and a half later, you have either an orange or half a grape-fruit. They limit the fruits because of the triglyceride levels and natural sugars in them. Then about 11 o'clock they put out a tremendous raw vegetable salad bar which is open till 3:30. And you can go and eat as much of that stuff whenever you want. Radishes, carrots, all the standard things. At 12:30, you have a vegetable soup that contains no oils or fats. Not even chicken broth. And they were great recipes. Roz continues to make them. Soups were either cold gaspacho, or yellow squash. You also had some sort of carbohydrate with it, rice, bulgar, kasha . . . Then you could continue to eat vegetables. You don't sit around and eat because there's classes going on and exercises, but it was there. At 4 or 4:30, you had some form of carbohydrate . . . half a baked potato or half a sweet potato. I think that was a great energy producer.

Then dinner would be the same salad bar, some type of main course,

Jack Fulton

some carbohydrate with vegetables. Beans or lentils; they had a great vegetarian chili. Pastas and sauces made from fresh tomatoes.

What do you do at home? Are you as strict as at Pritikin's?

No, because one of our children is home now, or you may have guests over. But you cook things the Pritikin way. And if Roz is making some other kind of potatoes, I'll have a plain baked potato. It's not *real hard*. It's surprising. There's no problem, if you want to do it.

One of the most important things at Pritikin for me was a lecture given by this Dr. Zifferblatt. He's a real interesting guy, real trim, but used to weigh 200 lbs. He explained the reactions in your body from sugar, caffeine, and smoking. Have you ever heard of the flight or fight syndrome? Well, I think it's the keynote to the Pritikin Center's philosophy. It deals with stress . . . When there was a cave man 2 million years ago and he had nothing in the world to worry about but what he was going to eat, he would go out from his cave with his club and walk by some bushes. The bushes would rattle. His club automatically comes up, his heart starts beating faster, he sweats, because he doesn't know if what's behind that bush is going to be *his* meal or if he's going to be *its* meal. That's stress. And the same thing happens to your body today. It's a miracle. The trouble is that when you're about to get into an automobile accident, that happens to you and when you get a telephone call from your wife that she's had a flat tire, the same mechanism works. The modern world puts so much stress on you . . . and it's good. Let me tell you, when you get that club up and you're ready to fight, you feel pretty good. When you have a cigarette, or a piece of sugar, the same system works in your body. Your pancreas secretes something that lowers the sugar rate over a period of time so that in an hour you start to go down, but you want another cup of coffee or another candy bar, or another cigarette, or you eat a Danish. Those things build up. And that's what aggravates stress. The stopping of the coffee first thing in the morning, the caffeine which triggers that same mechanism, lets you stop the cigarette, lets you stop the candy, lets you stop the drinking. And then at the same time exercising, which is burning up other stuff, you start to feel good. You start to feel good about yourself.

Do you have any friends who do the same type of thing or are you guys pretty much alone among your acquaintances?

The last thing Pritikin tells you is, "Look, we appreciate if you want to tell anybody about us. Give us their names. We'll send them some information and follow up on it. But we don't need any born-again Pritikinites. If you want to save yourself a lot of stress, don't start preaching." So, no, I don't go out and lecture . . . There is nothing worse than having someone telling you you're eating too much butter, you don't need that cupcake . . . So I don't discuss it with anybody. People tell me I look terrific. I really feel good. I'm going to spend my next 49 years not being stressed.

And with that, interview concluded, Don and I walked about 8 blocks to a small Vietnamese restaurant. We sat down and Don told the waiter, "The same as last time." The week before Don had handed him one of Pritikin's cards in Chinese saying, steamed rice and vegetables, no salt, no oil, no MSG . . . We soon had a delicious meal of crunchy vegetables and rice, with a few steamed prawns on top. □

For information on Pritikin diet, clinics or publications, write:

Pritikin Research Foundation
1910 Ocean Front Walk
Santa Monica, Calif., 90405

Roz Kahn

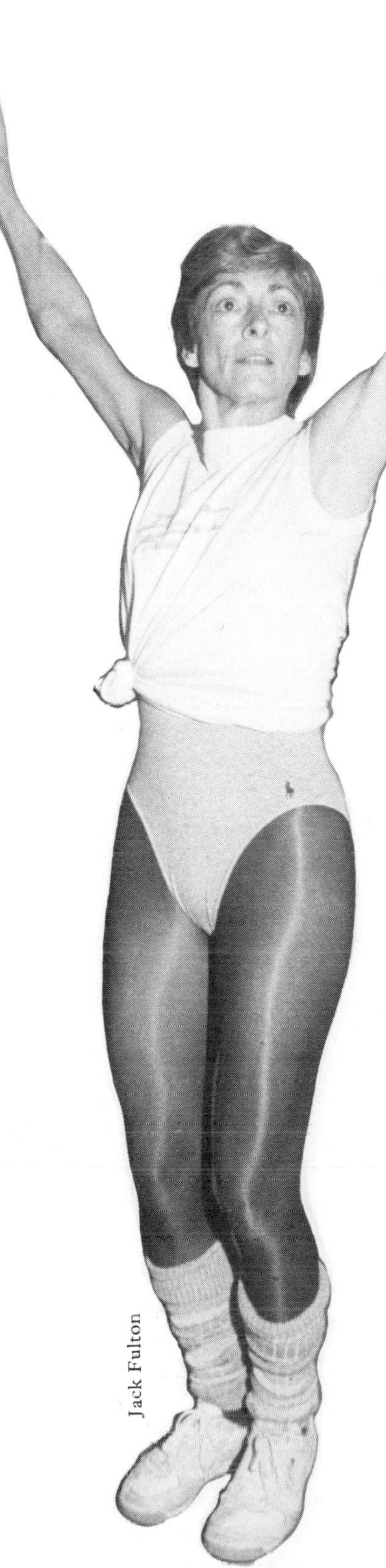
Jack Fulton

Roz Kahn was playing tennis one day when "... my body went one way and my knee another." For Roz, 50 and a new grandmother, it put an abrupt end to an extremely energetic athletic schedule: tennis three times a week, three weekly runs of 5-7 miles, and early morning aerobics classes two or three times a week.

Roz and Don (see p. 65) got married when they were students at the University of California at Berkeley. They have two sons and a daughter. When Roz was 40, in the mid-'70s, she went back to school at San Francisco State University, working toward a Master's degree in physical education. While attending State she taught beginning tennis and classes in field hockey.

As part of her Master's program she took classes in anatomy and physiology and learned a lot about the inner and outer workings of the body. Thus when she was injured she had a fairly good idea of just exactly what the damage was. After trying the typical non-surgical approaches to healing to no avail, Roz interviewed several orthopedic surgeons and finally settled on one who would perform arthroscopic surgery and allow her to remain awake through the operation.

Vital Statistics

Roz Kahn, 51
Date of Birth: June 7, 1934
Born: San Francisco, California
Height: 5'4½" **Weight**: 120
Job: Works in daughter's store *Robin's Nest* in Sonoma, California
Lives in: San Francisco, California
Activites: Walking, Nautilus, tennis

How did you hurt your knee?

I was playing tennis and went to get a very low shot. My body went one way and my knee pulled another. It was as though I was tripping on a cord. And I actually heard it and felt it rip.

I knew immediately in my own head that I had torn something. I thought it was going to be a cartilage and it was. Everybody said, "Oh, maybe it's your ligament." And I said, "No, there's no swelling."

What did you do?

Iced it. Elevation. Rested it. I sure didn't play tennis again. But I was convinced it wasn't going to heal by itself. After a couple of months, when it was painful just to walk, I went for surgery.

Describe what happens with arthroscopy. *(Arthroscopy refers to the use of a small sterile metal tube and fiber optic light source to look inside the body. Surgery is done through the arthroscope.)*

They drilled three holes in my knee. I had a spinal anesthetic because I wanted to be awake during the surgery. Two of the doctors told me they had seen people get up from the table screaming, writhing in pain, because of the tourniquet. But I felt I didn't want to be knocked out. So I went to someone who agreed with me.

As for the surgery itself—they lift both your legs up and immediately apply a tourniquet. It's bloodless surgery really. Then they drill the holes. I heard them drilling. They put two on the left side of the kneecap and one on the right one is for the light source, one is for a saline solution, the third for surgical instruments.

My body went one way and my knee pulled another. I knew immediately I had torn something.

Then they insert the little microscope. And that is thrown up on a screen. The doctor was wonderful. He said, "I want you to look up at the things I'm going to point out to you." And he pointed out the head of the femur. He showed me the patella. And he actually lifted the kneecap.

That's all in one shot?

Yeah. There's a fisheye lens. Really interesting. He said, "I want you to see what is giving you the trouble." Meantime, the solution washes everything so it sort of floats. It looks like the ocean with seaweed growing. And he said, "Here it is." He showed me the medial meniscus. It was as though I'd taken a piece of tissue paper and torn it. He said, "Every time you walk, this flaps." And he touched it with the arthroscope. I could see it flap. And I thought, "Oh, I must have been in a lot of pain." (*Laughter*) Then he said, "You have extremely strong ligaments." And he showed me my ligament. It's fascinating surgery.

Then he goes through the third hole with some kind of probe. It must have been sharp at the end of the probe, because he cut the meniscus. You take a piece of tissue paper and tear it but it doesn't tear all the way through. So he cut off the piece that was flapping. Pushed the rest of it back. That's the operation.

And now it's just healing?

Right. However, because I know what's in my knee, because I actually saw it, I don't think I'll ever run again. I think my running years are over. I think running could lead to arthritis. And because I'm looking ahead to my 60s and 70s, and I hope I make it...

Bobbie Kamler

Roz carrying 1984 Olympic torch through San Francisco

C'mon, 80s and 90s.

OK. I don't want arthritis. And I think this is the typical injury that could cause arthritis.

You know, when you're hurt, it seems like you're never going to get better and you always do.

You always do, but I think it's better to take it very slowly by not pushing anything. I'm taking very good care. I'd like to be very strong again. □

Leo Le Bon

Leo Le Bon came to America from Belgium on a slow freighter in 1959. A friend who knew the captain had promised him an easy job as ship's typist in return for free passage. But naturally, "The minute I got on board they put me in the hold with a crowbar to scrape the rust off the hull." After 6 months in New York, Leo got a driveaway car to the west coast and arrived in San Francisco with $50.

These days Leo runs an outfit called Mountain Travel, just outside Berkeley, California, in an old house which is breathtaking to enter. There are artifacts from all over the world on the walls: African masks, Pakistani jewelry, Tibetan thangkas, Berber saddlebags. One room is full of computers, with 25 full-time employees making reservations around the world. Mountain Travel specializes in "adventure travel," tours to the Himalayas, the Sahara, skiing in the Alps, climbing Fuji or Kilamanjaro, rafting down the Amazon.

Recently, to celebrate his 50th birthday, Leo organized an "Old Codgers" expedition where he and a group of friends over 50 trekked into the remote mountain valleys of the Hunza in the Western Karakoram in Pakistan.

Vital Statistics
Leo Le Bon, 51
Date of Birth: April 6, 1934
Born: Antwerp, Belgium
Height: 6'0" **Weight:** 175
Job: Travel executive
Lives in: Berkeley, California
Activities: Running, cycling, trekking, mountaineering, sailing

Nadia LeBon

Leo Le Bon amongst peaks north of Batura Glacier in the Western Karakoram in Pakistan in 1984

In 1963 the Sierra Club decided to organize some trips to Peru and Chile and they contacted me. I organized these, then some more trips to Europe and South America. Pretty soon I realized there was a demand for a new type of travel, the "outdoor" travel market. By 1967, I got together with 2 other guys and started organizing trips. We were all travelers and outdoors enthusiasts and we put together what we called our "dream trips." The first one was a Dhaulagiri/Annapurna trek in Nepal. When we got back, we printed up a small flyer: several more trips to Nepal, a backpack trip across Corsica, a climb of Mt. Kenya, a hiking trip in Iceland and a three week ski-tour across the Alps. And things took off.

How would you explain these treks? Just what is "adventure travel"?

Adventure is within. It is many things to many people. It's diverse. To one person it may be walking in the back alleys of a bazaar in Katmandu, to another person it may be climbing in the Himalayas. And yet to another it may be walking up and down a street in Berkeley. In the tourist sense, it's a new trend in recreation. It's a journey, a vacation—whether alone, with friends or an organized group—which combines a number of elements. Such as travel to remote places far from the standard tourist routes, places where there are limited or no facilities. The trip requires active physical participation through hiking, skiing, rafting, whatever it might be. And, I guess, above all, you have to be extremely flexible and willing to accept the unexpected.

You go on a 30-day trek, you come back totally revitalized. You're a new person.

You know, the difficult thing to explain about all this is that one is either in that state of mind or not. You have to define what kind of travel you're talking about. In the ordinary sense of the word, it means going on a bus tour of Europe or driving about the country in your car with the kids in the back or something like that. But if you're talking about "adventure travel," it means something entirely different. You see? It means hitchhiking. It means bumming your way around the world, sleeping in lofts or camping on the side of the road. Vagabonding, really. That's what it comes closer to. It's organized vagabonding. *(Laughter)*

I feel I have a calling, a long-term goal to reach out and spread the word. I just came back from this trip to Europe—mostly doing hardnose business in Belgium and Italy and New York. And you come back exhausted. Even if you stay in first-class hotels. You eat the hotel food—institutional food. And airports and taxis and big cities. You're exhausted. But you go on a 30-day trek, you come back totally revitalized. You're a new person.

You've seen that happen?

To thousands of people. People write me letters. This woman told me the other day, she grabbed my hand and looked me in the eye and said, "Leo, I have to tell you this. You've touched my life. You've changed me." Here she's a wealthy Jewish New York socialite. She goes on these expeditions and roughs it and sleeps in tents. And she says, "I can't believe I'm doing this!" She's wearing a 10-carat diamond worth $100,000. *(Laughter)*

When you first started doing it in the late '60s, was there any connection with the so-called "revolution" in those days and the spirit of adventure?

Not at the start, but later on those people came into it. The people we got at the beginning were mostly Sierra Club types. Outdoors persons, die-hards. Those people who were already converts. People who on the weekends would go walking or camping in the Sierras. Or hiking in Tilden Park or up on Mt. Tamalpais. We didn't have to explain too much to those people. In fact, they were just waiting for adventure travel to become available so they could go on these trips. Take your average doctor, lawyer or whatever. A businessman who is an active out-doors person . . . these people had no way to organize an expedition to the Himalayas. It was unheard of 25 years ago.

Do you travel a third or a quarter of the time still?

More or less.

So you're doing a lot of walking on those trips?

That's right.

Do you work out? Do you run?

I run, yeah. A little bit, but I've cut down on running. I don't think it's all that healthy for you. There's a lot of stress on your joints and bones. I find that it's not really necessary. I keep very active. I ski a lot. I ski hard downhill. I ski hard cross-country. My girlfriend and I go racing. Plus, we bicycle a lot. We go kayaking. We do some running. We play tennis.

Do runners or marathoners turn out to be in better shape than the average trekker?

They're tuned up for a tremendous output of energy in a very short time but it seems like they don't have the long-term stamina to walk for 20 days, 15 miles a day with a pack on your back up and down mountains. They can't handle that. They just want to go for a 2-hour run. So they've all had disappointments, these people. They were not prepared for the long haul. It's not just the short-term. They have to deal with clothing and food, with lodging and sleeping out, altitude problems, dietary problems, adverse weather conditions. It's entirely different. Number one, psychologically, you must be prepared. And physically you have to have that long-term stamina. So we're very skeptical when someone comes to us and their only fitness is distance running. It just doesn't work.

What was your Tibet trip like?

A journey into the unknown. The roof of the world. It's not as forbidden as some people imagine. It's not just all snow and ice and sub-zero temperatures. It's mysterious. It's a land of mystique. It's a land as it was. Of course, now with the Chinese occupation, it's totally different. It's very complex to answer what's Tibet like. It's arid. It's high altitude desert. The light is very intense. The atmosphere is

John Cleare

extremely dry. Powerful. It lends itself to out-worldly experiences because you're at 14,000 ft. Buddhism, of course, is the religion of Tibet and it's very much imbedded in the culture.

Personally, I'm very attracted to that other world of enlightenment, of philosophy, of abstraction. Once you've been to the Himalayas, it's hard not to go back there.

Although now Nepal has become very touristy. There are so many people going trekking. And you're so sheltered from all these outside influences. Now the food is well cooked, everything is western. You have good tents and sleeping bags, and you're not exposed to the real way Himalayan people travel. But if you would go on your own with just a pack over your shoulder and have to make do with whatever words you know and find shelter and trek and walk like the early explorers did, you'd have a totally different experience.

It's still there for you?

Absolutely. Nothing's changed really. Like these ski resorts you go to. We were skiing two days ago at Alpine Meadows. There's this groomed slope and everybody's up and down. And you go on the other side of the hill, and there are the enormous Sierras, untouched. □

Leo Le Bon rock climbing at Baggy Point, North Devon

Rod Lundquist

Lloyd Kahn, Jr.

Rod Lundquist won't know it until he reads this, but he was one of my heroes back in the '50s. Rod lived in Santa Cruz, California, in an old house he rented for $10 a month from an estate in probate. He was getting his Masters in English from San Jose State and surfing whenever he could. Not just "surfing," but systematically seeking out the biggest, fastest, scariest waves he could find. Rod grew up near Ocean Beach in San Francisco and was a champion high school freestyle swimmer.

In the '50s surfing was a far different sport. There were no rubber suits. Boards were balsa wood, not polyurethane foam. Waves were seldom crowded. Surfers were often frozen. But the surfer's mentality of the day didn't differ too much from nowadays–not exactly intellectual heavyweights. The physical conditioning of swimming and paddling, the sun, the thrills and speed of the waves, the negative ions produced such a state of well-being that most surfers were content to do just that–surf.

Not Rod. He was consumed with everything he did. He read voraciously. Shakespeare, Plato, Aristotle, Kant, Dostoevsky, Tolstoy . . . If you went by his house at midnight chances are he'd be wrapped up in a sleeping bag with tea and cinnamon toast and a heavy volume of some sort in his lap. He set up two big speakers and a turntable in the old house and the Beethoven symphonies would resound for blocks. He wrote poetry and essays and studied classical guitar. All feverishly.

Through it all, this minor madman was invariably amusing, stimulating and at times awesome. It was often "Well, what's Rod up to now?" After college and Santa Cruz, I lost track of him. I heard from friends that he'd given up surfing for hang gliding.

So one sunny morning I stopped in at his house in Santa Cruz–having seen him only once since the early '60s. The first thing I saw on going into his house was a picture on the wall of Rod in his hang glider at 5000 feet. When he saw me looking at it with more than passing interest he said, "Come on, I'll show you something." We went upstairs and with no discussion like "How've you been . . ." or "What have you been doing the last 25 years . . ." he pulled out a scrapbook of color photos and started flipping through the pages. "This is above the White Mountains . . . this one is in Spain last year . . ." Incredible vistas–above the ocean, over the Owens Valley, sunsets, intricate patterns from up high. And what was this shape in many of the pictures, a small black figure strapped in above the pilot? Rod's dog Duke! It turned out that Duke was Rod's occasional airborne companion, had no fear, loved flying–looked a lot like a dog hanging out a car window.

A few months later I went back to see Rod and, in spite of his protestations that "I don't work out, you know," picked up the threads of this adventurer still riding on the edge, only now on air currents instead of waves. "It's what I was always trying to do with surfing–fly."

Vital Statistics
Rod Lundquist, 51
Date of Birth: June 17, 1934
Born: San Francisco, California
Height: 5'10½" **Weight**: 180
Job: English instructor, Cabrillo College
Lives in: Santa Cruz, California
Activities: Hang gliding

(We're looking at a relief map of the Owens Valley in California.)

We used to take off here about halfway up the White Mountains, fly to the top and run the Whites, then turn the corner out here into Nevada and fly out there. That's where the cross-country records are made. It's very exciting flying because you get very high, 15-20,000 feet. You have to take oxygen. Two to three thousand feet over the terrain is a good flight around here. Down there, of course, the terrain is real high. White Mountain Peak is 14,200. Mt. Whitney is 14,400. Then you get another 3-4-5000 feet over the range because the thermals go real high. You do a lot of cruising typically between 13-16,000 feet.

At what point do you start taking oxygen?

Well, the Air Force recommends 12 but most of us don't worry about it until 15 or 16.

It's probably like running in a high altitude.

I suppose. It's not just your lungs, your blood has to change its chemistry, you know? And it's a little dangerous to screw around at the limit because one of the first things that goes is

Terry Ebert

Rod aloft with his dog Duke.

your judgment. Then after that you're likely to pass out. I don't think we've had anybody killed from it but we've had some people scare the shit out of themselves.

Do you hit the ground hard when landing?

Well, you don't come down that fast but with the new gliders you land with a fairly fast forward speed. I've had serious problems landing these new gliders because you have to flare the wings at just the right moment. You're coming in at a little over 20 mph and if there's wind, that's fine. You're flying into the wind and the wind speed cancels out your air speed so you land at 10 or 15 and that's no problem. But if there's no wind, the way you stop the glider is just the way you see birds land, you have to wait until just the exact moment of proper air speed, not ground speed, but air speed. And then you flare the wing real hard.

With a control, you mean?

You throw the bar out. And if you do it too soon, you'll pop 30 feet into the air and stall up there and crash land. If you do it too late, of course, nothin' happens, you just bong in forward. So on new gliders people bong in quite a bit actually.

How long have you been doing it?

7 years now, since 1977.

Are the new gliders like new surfboards, a real improvement in technology since you started?

Oh, yeah. They go through phases. You'll get a jump ahead, then a few years of refinement where things are staying pretty much the same but they're just refining that improvement. And then somebody will come up with another idea.

Do you carry a parachute?

Yeah, you have a parachute on your stomach usually. I've never used it. I hope I never do.

You got injured one time.

I dislocated my shoulder because I took off without clipping in. That is, I forgot to fasten the carabiner on my harness to the hangstrap on the glider. I just ran off this cliff holding on to the glider and, having no control, dove in from about forty feet. As I went through the bars, one arm got tangled up and jerked five inches out of the socket. It hurt a little worse than childbirth.

How did you feel when you went up again?

Well, I was a little edgy. I kept thinking, in another month, I'll fly or in another 6 weeks I'll fly. Then, one day I just said, "I'm going flying." So it was a little sooner than I'd expected. Then I did a couple of bong-ins on these new gliders with the fast landings and hurt it again. I got real concerned and realized I had to get my landing technique sorted out.

When did you quit surfing?

The same time I started flyin'. I went hang gliding and never went surfing again.

Why did you get into this? Just read about it?

About 15 years ago, I found an old book in my garage about the early days of flight, written in the '30s, and it talked about the early hang gliders. They had hang gliders before the Wright Brothers—before airplanes. They weren't exactly like these, but they were gliders that you crawled around on and used weight to control flight. There was a guy named Lillienthal that had flights up to 20 minutes and hundreds of feet. There was a guy here in Santa Clara County named Montgomery who was flying a hang glider in 1887. He had a pilot (an acrobat from a circus) who called himself Professor Lanier and wore tights. And they did balloon drops from 4000 feet. They both got killed finally.

When was this?

Well, their *big* flights were around the turn of the century, 1901-2. They did a balloon drop over the Santa Clara County Fairgrounds and the Professor killed himself because a rope got hung up on the balloon. When they cut loose it damaged part of the glider. He waved to the crowd as he went in.

How did you first get into it?

I actually drew up a plan for a hang glider that was pretty primitive but it might have worked. I figured if they could do that way back then... It looked much more like an airplane than our hang gliders do, this one I drew. I took it down to a boat builder I knew to get it built but he was always drunk and I was always broke so we never got around to it. Then when the new ones started 10 or 12 years ago, I did something very smart actually. I said, "OK, this is very exciting. I'll wait till 1000 guys break their backs on these things and then I'll start flyin' 'em."

That was mid-'70s or something? I didn't realize it was so new.

This new modern era is only about 10 years old. So then I went and

No matter how much you want to fly, your body is a little apprehensive at first.

took lessons. Anybody who is gonna start should definitely go to a first-rate school and take a lot of lessons. It's very dangerous to learn on your own. Fatalities are way down now. I think we only have about 4 or 5 people killed a year in this country.

How many hang gliders are there?

I think about 20,000.

So you like being up in the air?

Yeah, I really wanted to fly. When I was a surfer 20 years ago I used to dream about flying once a month and it was just like hang gliding. I was laying out flying.

No fear?

Sure, no matter how much you want to fly, your body is a little apprehensive at first. You train on the beach, typically, or a little hill, and you only fly 4 feet off the ground on your first flight. Then you fly 6 ft., 8 ft., 10 ft., 12 ft. As you get a little higher, you're getting a little more apprehensive. But then at a given point, you realize that the higher you are the safer you are. It's the ground that's gonna hurt you. The air never hurt anybody. It's the first quarter inch of earth that you have to watch out for. So at your higher altitude you breathe easier. Then typically there's another kind of shock when you first go off something real high. I got to flying 40 or 50 feet high on the beach there and felt rather good about that. By then you have your landing and takeoff technique pretty well worked out. So then you go up to something 3-400 feet high, or in my case it was about 1000 feet high. And that's a bit of a gas the first couple of times you do that. But then again you get very used to that and realize the higher you are the better off you are.

That's when you get real excited?

You get quite excited just being that high off the ground and being in control.

You don't just continually think about a wing falling off? That's what I think about in a light airplane.

Well, wings don't fall off light airplanes, of course. If you're really going to think about safety, on a big airplane you're dependent on hundreds of people doing everything right to stay alive. Where this thing is pretty much your own thing. There are very few, if any, mechanical failures anymore.

Is there any comparision with surfing?

Yeah, it's like surfing 5,000 foot waves.

So you get kind of the same feeling?

You go through several phases. There's your training period and then you get into soaring which is typically ridge soaring. There are two ways to stay up in a hang glider, either ridge soaring or thermal flying. Ridge soaring is just wind blowing over a ridge. It may be just a little beach ridge 30 feet high or it may be a 10,000 foot mountain. The wind goes up and if the ridge is steep enough and the wind is strong and is coming at the right angle, you can stay up by floating around. There's a lot of soaring ridges that range from 100 yards long to a couple miles long. And you can stay up as long as you stay within the confines of the ridge. You can float around indefinitely. The other way to stay up is from thermal activity which occurs as a result of the uneven heating of the earth's surface. There are hot spots on the surface of the earth and cold spots. Hot spots being bare, stony spots and the cooler spots being more covered with water or trees. These hot spots warm the adjacent air. The warmer air eventually breaks off the ground and rises and colder air sinks to fill in the vacated space. The rising air tends to be concentrated in what we call thermals which can range anything from 30-900 feet across. The sinking air tends to be more widely distributed, it's not as violent, although there can be areas of very rapid sink as well. If you see birds circling and going up without flapping their wings, they're riding thermals. So you go off to some hill or mountain and fly off, you try and catch thermals and then you circle them. And they take you up. That is really what most advanced flyers are interested in these days. Thermals can be quite powerful. In a good thermal the glider goes up 500 feet a minute. A very good thermal will be 1000 feet a minute, or dynamite thermals, 2-3000 feet. That's very rapid ascent.

What do hang gliders think of the ultra-light powered airplanes? Is that a natural transition?

No. There are very few people who fly both. It's like the difference between, I suppose, speedboats and small sailboats. The one is a sport, an athletic activity. And the other is a mechanical hobby.

It *is* athletic? You use certain muscles . . .

Oh, yeah. You're using your body to turn the airplane. Landing and taking off require a good deal of coordination. In thermals you're getting into a considerable amount

The only alternatives, or counter-cultures, you had in 1952 were the Hell's Angels, or you could be a drunk or you could go with the corporations.

of turbulence. Every time a thermal hits you from one side, it wants to roll the glider the other way and you have to cantilever your body. You struggle pretty violently sometimes. And thermals are not just perfectly shaped. The up and down air is mixed around in strange shapes. So you're pretty busy in thermals. You can work up a good sweat. You get down low where the altitude really matters and you gotta make all your moves well or you're on the ground. So thermals are a pretty good workout.

You have to be in some kind of shape to do it?

Yeah. To be a good flier, you have to be in decent shape. If you lay off for awhile and then start flying thermals again, you're sore and exhausted when you finish.

How did you decide to take the dog flying?

Well, other guys had flown dogs before me. And Duke was always there. In the very beginning when I was training down in Marina, he was always running underneath me. I'd fly back and forth down the hill there, and he'd be running underneath like a shadow. So a friend of mine who was a sailmaker had built a harness for his dog and actually it didn't fit so well so he wanted to build another. And it turned out the harness fit my dog better than his.

What is it like flying in Europe?

Much more interesting than flying here. Here you typically go inland for the super flying. And inland, man, is bozo land. It's just all these grunthead cowboys. And it's *dull*, man. The towns are all franchised out. If there were just a bunch of old desert rats, it would be colorful, but everybody under 50 is wearin' their Sizzler uniform.

When you go to Europe, you move 200 miles and you're in a different civilization. It's really fun . . . Whereas here you just go up into some dry foothills and it's 90-100° and there's just nothin' to do on the ground but kick dust. I get bored fast. I'm going to Morocco this fall . . . They have some big, big mountains there.

(Then we started talking about surfing in the '50s.)

Yeah, surfing was a good thing, wasn't it? For me, it was a vehicle out of a really tedious society. The only alternatives, or counter-cultures, you had in 1952 were the Hell's Angels, or you could be a drunk or you could go with the corporations. Those were your options. Then surfing came along which was new, then. It gave you a whole other time scheme and set of motivations.

I was driving along this morning thinking it's not special anymore. It's so commercialized.

It's like volleyball. It's just one more organized sport. But at the time it was unknown what the limits were, what it was all about. It made these weird demands on your time, you had to be there when the surf was there, it dislocated you from the world of work. You couldn't ever take a steady job and you couldn't plan your social life two days ahead of time. Anyone invited you to a party, you'd say, "Well, I'll *try* and make it." And you'd never plan a party yourself, ever. Because it meant you had to be home when maybe the surf was up. We were that obsessed with it.

That was the result. That wasn't *why* you surfed. You surfed and that was part of surfing.

Yeah, but somehow the appeal of surfing and that monomania involved was more exciting to us than all of the strictures and structure and incentives and frustrations of what our peers were up to. From high school on we were being separated. We were also on our own toot. And it remains that way even today for high school kids. It's a way out. It's a period in life in high school when a lot of sorting out is going on and you're being conditioned rather heavily to take shape for the corporations. If you have talent, at least, the corporations pick you up. If you haven't any talent, then you're a failure. Some of us weren't that convinced that the corporation's blessings were so marvelous. There were all sorts of obvious reasons to go that way because that's where the material rewards were.

But you discovered that time was your most valuable commodity. That money is time actually, rather than the opposite. I didn't ever think I'd grow up and be a surfer. I was *astounded* in my early 30s when I found myself still surfing. And I made various attempts to get uptown but I was always thwarted because whatever happened there wasn't enough fun. So I'd head back to the beach again. □

Denise Phillips

Don Manoukian

One of my good friends at Stanford came from Denver and every spring I'd go home with him on Easter vacation. Six of us would get in a car and share gas and driving, most of the others getting out in Nevada or Wyoming en route to Denver. One of the riders was Donald Manoukian, star football player, heavyweight wrestler, weightlifter, raconteur and good-will ambassador. When we'd get into Reno, everyone *knew him, he was a hometown hero; riding down the streets felt like being with the mayor. And best of all, Manouk would pay for his portion of the gas by having us over to his house for dinner before we continued on our way. The table would be heaped with Armenian foods: dolma, pilaf, kufta, hummus, all foods we'd never heard of before, and all delicious. His mother, a warm and wonderful woman, loved to cook and loved to feed people. (Don's sons now bring* their *friends over to Mama's to eat).*

I lost track of Manouk until last year when I called him up. "Kahn, you little fart, how're you doing?" Since he'd gotten out of Stanford he'd played for the Oakland Raiders, been a professional wrestler for ten years, a disc jockey in Hawaii (The Bruiser Hour)*, and was now in the real estate and land development business in Las Vegas and Reno. He and his wife Carol came by our house in Bolinas one night for dinner. We intended to do this interview then, but with kids climbing all over him, reminiscing with Carol (a San Francisco girl) about the good old days in the city by the bay, eating pizza and drinking wine, we never got to the tape recorder. So this was done over the phone one day when Don was in Las Vegas. He's now 51, and just passed a physical for a million-dollar life insurance policy, including a 26-minute treadmill test.*

Vital Statistics

Donald Manoukian, 51
Date of Birth: June 9, 1934
Born: Merced, California
Height: 5'8" **Weight**: 240
Job: Real estate development and investment
Lives in: Reno, Nevada
Activities: Racquetball, weight lifting, swimming

When did you start lifting weights?

In '48-'49. It was frowned upon by 99% of the coaches then. They claimed it would make you muscle-bound, that it would do a lot of negative things. Of course, over the years, it's been proved they were medieval thinkers.

After Stanford you wrestled professionally for a while.

That's right. Immediately after school I went into professional wrestling. I wrestled from '57 to '67. That was my source of income except for 1960. I signed with the Oakland Raiders and played the first year of the American Football League.

How did you like pro football?

Oh, I loved it but at that time they just weren't paying any money. Unless you were fresh out of college and had a big name that would help draw. By then I'd been out of college three years and we were pretty old hat. So I played football for them that one year and Jim Otto, the offensive center and I and a kid named Wayne Hawkins, the other guard, we were on the first All-Pro team for the Raiders. But after that I just kissed it off and wrestled full time. You couldn't really wrestle part time and be depended upon to show up all over the country as you were expected to. Because hey, you get going good and everybody starts to know you and recognize you and then you disappear for 6 months playing football.

How'd you like the wrestling?

Oh, it was great. I got to travel, primarily to Japan where I was received very well. It was just an experience I'll never forget. The most memorable times of my life were in Japan.

What about working in Hawaii?

That was about the same time. I would winter in Hawaii. I was a D.J. I had the prime time driving-home hours, the Bruiser Hour. And that's where my first son Dick was born, in 1963.

And then you eventually came back to Reno and got into the real estate business?

Well, I went to graduate school of business at the University of Hawaii and got my credentials and then got my broker's license while I was still wrestling. So I was preparing all along for the day when I would ultimately get off the road.

What do you do now as far as working out?

I try to work out every day—either play racquetball for an hour or I will lift certain days. I may have two serious days of weightlifting and I

Victor Andersson

What I consider heavy is when I lift over 400 lbs. When you get to be about 50 you can't lift heavy every week.

may also go and play a few games. I try to run, I try to play racquetball every day. It's something I have to do to keep the knees in condition. You'd think alternating and laying off for a while would make you last longer but that's not the case. You've got to play it all the time.

What's your attitude toward priorities, you know, working out versus a busy schedule?

I can't handle a busy schedule if I'm not in good physical condition. So the conditioning part of my existence is very important. In fact just as I'll go to the office early and get the paper work out of the way and make appointments for the rest of the day, I'll make an appointment for myself at the gym. I promise myself so much time for working out. I normally start my day off at 6:30 in the morning, going to the gym. I'll hit the Jacuzzi, shave in the sauna, loosen up a little bit and get all cleaned up for the day. Then at the end of the day I'll work out. I have a very flexible schedule where I can work out virtually any time I want.

Tell me about your fitness center in Vegas.

It's called the Springmountain. We own the building and we run the business. We have about 1200 members, and it's a 36,000 sq. ft. building: 15 racquetball courts, a basketball gymnasium, women's aerobics classes and a full Nautilus fitness center.

Are there other ones in Vegas that big?

They have one here that's really gigantic. They have a running track on the inside, 21 racquetball courts, a dining room with a bar. A food center, a pro shop, the whole thing.

Are the members mostly full-time residents?

Well, Vegas is pretty transient. There are the people who fantasize getting into condition and then find out it's a lot of work after they buy the membership. At our club we have pretty serious recreational athletes. The other club is quite a bit different from ours. I mean, they're sort of jet-setters, you know, the guys that buy the $200 warm-up clothes and never break a sweat. They sit around with gold necklaces and have a few drinks and bullshit the young broads.

When you're lifting weights do you have a routine?

I have a pretty regular routine, but of course there are variations. I'll do conditioning most of the time and about every two or three weeks I'll lift heavy. I'll go close to maximum in certain lifts.

What's that in bench pressing?

Most of the time when I'm training I stay under 400 lbs. What I consider heavy is when I go over 400 lbs. When you get to be about 50 you can't lift heavy every week. Your muscles can stand it but you run into tendonitis. If you don't warm up or you get a little injury, you just don't respond as quickly as you used to and it interrupts your next few weeks of training. So it's better to just get the high reps with the lower weights and get the real good conditioning. Before, I'd just jump in with 300 or 350, grab it the first thing, now I warm up with lighter weights and do more reps. I can still go up heavy but I've got to prepare much better.

What do you press? Just standing and pressing up over your head?

I don't do the military press any more because of the obvious reason, which is damage to the lower back. So at this point I do those lifts but just light standing reps. I don't try to max out at all. Bench pressing is pretty safe, you can control the weight better and you don't have a real critical balance where the fulcrum point is in your lower back which, as you know, is the nemesis of all athletes.

How about squats?

I'll do some very light squats but my legwork is in the running when I play racquetball. I'll use the machines and I'll do some extensions and then reverse bicep leg curls, just to strengthen the joints. But my legs haven't gone down in size very much and they maintain definition; they let me do what I want to do to play pretty competitive racquetball. For that insurance policy, they put me through all the obvious tests, including a 26-minute stress test on the tread-mill which was quite unusual—they'd never seen a stress test with somebody of my age, weight and height. I passed it with flying colors and they couldn't deny me. You know there's a certain amount of it that's got to be genetic. I always had endurance.

Has your weight been pretty constant through the years?

No. It's varied. Off and on I've gone up to 250-260. You know when I was lifting real heavy. Now I've targeted a realistic plateau of what I want to be at a given age. I was right at 237 this morning; by the first of the year I want to be at 230.

Can you eat as much as you want?

No, no. I like beer very much and if I want to lose weight, I can't drink beer, because then you nibble: You take a little cheese, a little salami. I don't eat a great deal at one time. I just don't have the capacity to sit down and gorge anymore where, before, you could knock off, you know, a couple of steaks, salads and a loaf of bread. I can't do that and I don't want to do that anymore. Your body automatically rejects it at a time in life when there's just no way you can burn it all off. So it's a concentrated effort to maintain the weight and it's not an easy thing.

What's the name of your company?

Manoukian-Ribeiro Realty and Investments but the main company is Johnny Ribeiro, Builder Inc. Johnny, my partner, is the guy that makes it all work. He's a year ahead of the rest of the world. He's exceptional. His buildings win architectural awards. There's a lot of pride of ownership in all the property.

What happened to you guys in the recession? Did it effect your sales?

We had very steady solid growth during 1979 through 1982. It was hard on us like it was on everybody but we were on pretty solid footing in having properties that we had developed over the years that carried the weaker ones. We continue to

build and go ahead, like what we always say is, it's too late to become a brain surgeon, right? (*Laughter*) So we just got to do what we know. Just because it's tough, we can't quit; we just have to find a more resourceful way of doing it.

How big is the piece you're working on now?

It's a 118-acre project at McCann airport in Las Vegas. It used to belong to Howard Hughes' personal estate.

What are you going to do on it?

We're building 1,600,000 square feet.

Jesus.

Well, we build it in stages, we don't do it all at once. We'll build a couple of 40,000 foot buildings. When we lease those out we may have between 15 or 20 tenants in there—office and warehousing space combination. Then when we get it about half built we break ground on the next and we just keep going.

Big-time building.

Well, today, we have built about 2 million square feet in Las Vegas and 2 million square feet in Reno. We have our own property management company and our own landscaping crews that maintain all the property. If we do happen to sell a building within a park, we maintain control of landscaping and overall maintenance.

It sounds like a great partnership.

We put the relationship to the test in the last few years. You know it's easy to be partners when you make a lot of money and there's no problem but when you really have to struggle and things aren't very rosy, it puts everybody to the test, and we came through with flying colors. We have perfect rapport. □

Annabel Marsh

George Kruse—Greyhound

I'd have oatmeal and cinnamon toast and orange juice, or eggs and hash browns, pancakes, a tuna sandwich with a milkshake, hot fudge sundaes. We were ravenous!

On a cold April morning in 1984, Annabel Marsh set out on a run in Boston. Four months, 3,261 miles, 12 pairs of shoes and 494 chocolate chip cookies later, Annabel, age 61, and her running pal Caroline Merrill, age 42, crossed the Golden Gate Bridge amidst banners, flowers, ribbons, and champagne. 1984, the first year for the women's Olympic marathon, was also the first year any woman ever ran across the entire United States. Annabel will be listed in the Guinness Book of World Records, Sports Edition, *as the oldest woman to run across America.*

Now that she's back, Annabel still runs 50-60 miles a week. Her new goal is to break four hours in the marathon.

Where did the idea come from to run across America?

I was running in the park one day with Caroline and she said, "I've just written my mother and father an anniversary card and told them that when they celebrate their 50th anniversary, I'll run home to Michigan and help them celebrate." I said, "Great! I'll go with you." I'd been thinking about doing a transcontinental run for years. One thing led to another and before we knew it we had maps all over the living room floor. Instead of just Michigan, it was going to be cross-country. And we decided to do it during the 1984 Olympics; since this was the first year for the women's marathon it would be our little celebration of that. We wrote 49 letters to corporations all over America, and Greyhound was the first one to agree to sponsor the trip.

How did you train?

I did circuit training three times a week, a gradual buildup of mileage. For six months before we left I did 30 mile-a-day weeks, one week out of four. Just like we were going to do on the trip, 15 miles in the morning and 15 in the afternoon. 180 miles a week. Then it became one week out of three. Then every other week. But I never put them all together, back-to-back, until we started on the run.

Why did you start in Boston?

We had wanted to start out the trip with the Boston Marathon, but we couldn't qualify. Our times are too slow. I mean, we're 10-minute milers. We're the back-of-the-pack people, in the last third of the runners in races. So we started at the Greyhound terminal in Boston, and a Greyhound employee played the *Star-Spangled Banner* on his trumpet. We had a police escort for the first mile and Greyhound videotaped us for the first 15. It was a lot of fun.

Didn't you have some bad weather when you started?

It rained 21 out of the first 35 days. The trees were still bare back there and it was just raining, cold and bleak. Our third day out, after just about an hour of running, we were soaked through. We spotted this cafe and thinking a cup of coffee sounded good, we went in. They had a pot-bellied stove and we changed our wet clothes and draped them over chairs, had coffee and donuts, and waited out the rain. The first week we went through 27 pairs of socks.

We were in Pennsylvania a couple of weeks. That was our longest state. But you know, it was the people all along the way who really made the trip. Greyhound would send a press kit into an area right before we got there, and as a result, when people would see us on the road, they knew who we were. In Pennsylvania they brought us maple syrup and maple sugar candy; in other towns they'd bring homemade cookies and donuts. Some people even tried to give us money. It was great support. I think we thought we were just gonna do this thing for our own self-satisfaction. That's really all we intended to do.

What did you eat?

Everything in sight! Everything we could lay our hands on. We had a support van that was always 2½ miles ahead of us, and we'd stop often for snack food like cookies, raisins, bananas, candy, anything we could eat quickly. After our first 15 miles in the morning, we'd go to a restaurant. I'd have oatmeal and cinnamon toast and orange juice, or eggs and hash browns, pancakes, a tuna sandwich with a milkshake, hot fudge sundaes. We were ravenous! For dinner, sometimes we went to a nice restaurant, sometimes just diners because they were across the street and handy. Actually they had pretty good food. I had never really been in a diner before; they don't

Vital Statistics

Annabel Marsh, 62
Date of Birth: May 31, 1923
Born: Hampshire, Illinois
Height: 5'3" **Weight:** 114
Job: Retired
Lives in: San Francisco, California
Activities: Running, golf

We hit the wide open spaces . . . in Nebraska . . . Now we were beginning to see sagebrush and huge cattle farms. Rattlesnakes.

seem to have them out West. They look like old railroad cars.

How much liquid did you drink a day?

Gallons and gallons. We tried to drink a good 8-10 ounces of water every 2½ miles. In the morning, we had a cup of coffee. Caffeine is good for runners because it frees the fatty acids and you can run on that and save carbohydrates. Plus the smell of fresh coffee brewing in the morning is always a good thing to wake up to. Then I'd have a beer every night. It never tasted so good! When I was starting to get cramps in my hand at one point I called our podiatrist, Dr. Richard Blake, in San Francisco and he said, "Are you drinking beer?" I said, "Yes, one at the end of the day's run." He said, "Drink two and if that doesn't help, drink one during your break." See, beer has a lot of electrolytes and it replaces many of the minerals you're losing through perspiration.

Did you take electrolyte drinks?

No. We could get enough with our beer and our bottled mineral water. We did take vitamins though.

How about injuries?

We used the Osler method to prevent dehydration and injury. That's where you run 17 minutes and walk 3. Or any variation on that. In the hills in Pennsylvania and the rolling dairy farms of New York and Massachusetts we were unable to do that successfully. But once we got to Ohio and it was flat lands, we did that consistently then. We had blisters the first few weeks, I think because of the rain and our feet were wet a lot. Caroline was having trouble with shin splints, but she had those before we left. We had sore feet. And Achilles tendons. But we did this deep icing thing. You fill a big bucket with ice and put your feet in up to the knees for about 20 minutes every night. We called it "The Torture Chamber."

Did you ever think about quitting?

No. Not once. We always thought we would make it. We always felt positive. We met up with a sports psychologist in Ohio who told us if we had made it this far we would surely make it the rest of the way. So we felt pretty confident going into Iowa. Then it was such a thrill to cross the Mississippi because it felt like we were getting out West then. In Nebraska when we first caught sight of the Rocky Mountains, that was really exciting and kept us going through that long flat part of the country.

Was it getting hot by this time?

We were soaking wet with sweat by 6:30 in the morning. But we just kept throwing water on ourselves. And we wore these Sahara hats, with flaps in the back like the French Foreign Legion. When it really got hot, I'd put a wet sponge and ice cubes in my bra, and that helped. The afternoons got up into the high 80s and 90s in Nebraska, but that wasn't anything compared to Nevada heat.

We hit the wide open spaces where the terrain started changing in Nebraska. Up to that time we were more or less in civilization. Now we were beginning to see sagebrush and huge cattle farms. Rattlesnakes. We couldn't even get into the bushes in Nebraska because of the rattlesnakes. In Utah, there was a beetle migration. We heard there was a two-yard swath, six inches deep of beetles up ahead and we thought, how are we ever going to get through? They'll be crawling up our legs. But by the time we got there, the worst of it had passed, and we could step around them. But when the trucks came by they would spatter us with them. We had all kinds of bugs. Grasshoppers. We hit a town in Colorado two days after the mosquitoes hatched. You went out that door without insect repellant and you were covered.

The scariest part was an electrical storm in Nevada. I thought it was my last day on earth. The lightning came down right next to us on the road. Then it turned to hail. We flagged down a truck driver and when we jumped in he said, "What are you two doing out here in this storm?" "We're running across the United States," we told him. "You must be kidding."

This was really a trip though the heartland, wasn't it?

I felt really proud to be an American. I think we forget, living in an urban area, that the backbone of this country is in rural America. We ran right through Cleveland, our largest city, but for the most part we stayed in small towns. Mom and Pop motels. We liked that because they took a real interest in what we were doing. The people were friendly. They'd come out and ask for our autographs, take our pictures, bring us food. A lot of elderly people came out to greet us. I remember particularly one old lady in Ohio. She was standing there with a little bag of donuts, saying, "Oh I was so afraid I'd miss you. I read

Mark Duran–Greyhound

Running mate Caroline Merrill and Annabel soaking their legs in buckets of ice water. They did this every night after their daily 30 miles to reduce swelling and promote healing.

about you in the paper yesterday. I can't do what you're doing because I have arthritis in the knee. But you, you're doing it for me." We began to have a sense of responsibility, that we were doing this for everyone else who couldn't do it. It was very heartwarming.

How did it feel to reach California?

It was great to be home. The Sierras were just gorgeous. But you know, the funny thing about that last week, our feet got sore. A blister returned on the same spot that I hadn't had the whole trip, Caroline's shin splints started acting up, like we were now allowing ourselves to feel everything. We thought we'd have to crawl over the bridge. But coming across the Golden Gate was, of course, the climax of the whole trip. Greyhound had been there a couple of days in advance and arranged our homecoming. And the *Examiner* had a story about us the Sunday before we got there. So there were quite a few people to greet us. We started to cross. People were carrying flowers and champagne and grabbing at us. Two of our friends were holding a ribbon to mark the finish line. It was really a thrill. The inner satisfaction. The one moment—that one glorious, wonderful moment when you cross the finish line—and you know it's over. You've accomplished a goal. □

Doug McConnell

Doug McConnell has a Masters degree in political science from Rutgers. He has been a teacher intern on the Navajo Indian reservation in Arizona, was assistant director of the Institute of Ecology in Alaska, did communications projects for the governor of Alaska, worked on a special project for the Carter administration on coal mining, has worked for KTLA-TV in Los Angeles, WDZ-TV in Boston and KING-TV in Seattle.

These days he's co-host of Pacific Currents, *a popular Saturday night TV show on KPIX in San Francisco. He's handsome, athletic, bright and personable. With all that going for him, and such an interesting past, you'd think he'd be dying to talk about himself. Not so. He's practically bursting to talk about someone else entirely–Nicholas McConnell, age 1½.*

Our usual routine is that Nicholas wakes up, without exception, between 6:30 and 7:00. I'm not by nature an early morning person, but I've become one. So I go in and we play around in the crib for awhile. Then the two of us go into the bathroom, and I take a shower and he plays with the shampoo. Then I take him down and feed him. We sit and watch the CBS Morning News. It has to be CBS. *(Laughter)* By then, it's time to go wake mommy. Then mommy's got him for the rest of the day and I zip off to work.

What do you do as far as working out?

I try to get about an hour in every day doing something. I've always been involved in sports and physical things. I just have this habitual need to work out. Even when I travel–if I can't do anything else, I'll at least run. When I'm here in town, I'll lift weights 3 or 4 times a week and run on alternate days.

Lately, the greatest times I've had exercising are when I take Nicholas hiking on weekends. We go quite a bit. It gives my wife some free time. We started hiking together when he was 8 days old. I put him in the Snuggly and we hiked for a couple of hours. We gradually extended the time as he got older and able to be away from mom longer.

He wants to see everything now, so he's out of the Snuggly and into a little backpack. It's so great. Wonderful times for me! That connection with him–of all the things I do, those times with him are the best.

Do you think people appearing on TV pay extra attention to diet and health?

You're judged so much by your physical appearance. TV is sort of the land of the young and beautiful. I think it's going to be less that way as the years go by because the baby boom generation is getting older and we're going to be more accepting of older faces on the air. But I think people also expect you to look as good as you can, and to be as natural as possible. So there's extra pressure to stay in shape, yeah.

Describe your program and what you do.

It's a half hour magazine-formatted TV show. Usually 3 stories every week. Anywhere from real serious topics–really controversial topics–to light, frivolous, empty-headed topics. I'm co-host of the show and I produce stories. Which means I create ideas and then line up stories and go out and shoot them with our camera crew. Then I come back and review the tapes and I write the scripts, etc.

How is it being up against *Solid Gold* and *Wheel of Fortune?*

Wheel of Fortune runs over all of its competition, basically. So in terms of ratings we're Number 2 in our time slot there on Saturday night. For our show, which still tries to do sort of meaty topics, it's tough to succeed on a Saturday night at 7 o'clock when most people are ready for drugs, sex, rock and roll, or family entertainment. I feel good about what we've done. We've beat the odds, at least, in terms of ratings.

How do you balance work with the other important facets of your life?

I like to exercise but I have never killed myself at it. My work is important, but I also don't want to ruin my family because I'm working myself to death either. I try to find some kind of balance but at the same time continue to change, continue to grow, try new things and on and on. I would like to try some major physical adventure. I don't know what, but I need to do something just for the hell of it. Maybe walk across the country or something. □

Vital Statistics

Doug McConnell, 40
Date of Birth: April 30, 1945
Born: Gridley, California
Height: 5'11" **Weight**: 170
Job: TV producer, reporter
Lives in: San Francisco, California
Activities: Weight lifting, running, hiking

Jack Fulton

Roger Minkow

Roger Minkow is a man of many talents. An MD specializing in emergency medicine with a special interest in plastic surgery, Roger is also an artist whose drawings have appeared on the covers of several magazines, a car restorer, a rock and roll musician and designer of a variety of athletic devices, including the Upper Body Machine, *used by the 1984 Olympic men's gymnastics team and the Dallas Cowboys.*

When Roger began his medical practice, he sometimes worked 100-hour weeks. "I didn't realize how far I'd slipped until I saw a picture taken on a return trip to Norway. There I was, carrying a knapsack, just as I'd done 10 years before. But instead of looking lean and athletic, I had a small but very noticeable pot belly. Pathetic."

"I began working out with weights in 1977 and combined this with some gymnastics exercises. I worked towards doing a 'front lever'—something I'd always wanted to do in high school, but never could. I made a bet with a friend that I'd be able to do the move in one year. Three months later, I could do it."

Roger has two machines in the living room of his 2-story Victorian home. He works out 3-4 times a week with a group of friends.

Don Silverek

Roger and Heidi Minkow and their children, Katie and Ben

Vital Statistics

Roger Minkow, 40
Date of Birth: March 3, 1946
Born: New York, New York
Height: 5'9½" **Weight:** 150
Job: Emergency physician
Lives in: Petaluma, California
Activites: Weight training

Don Silverek

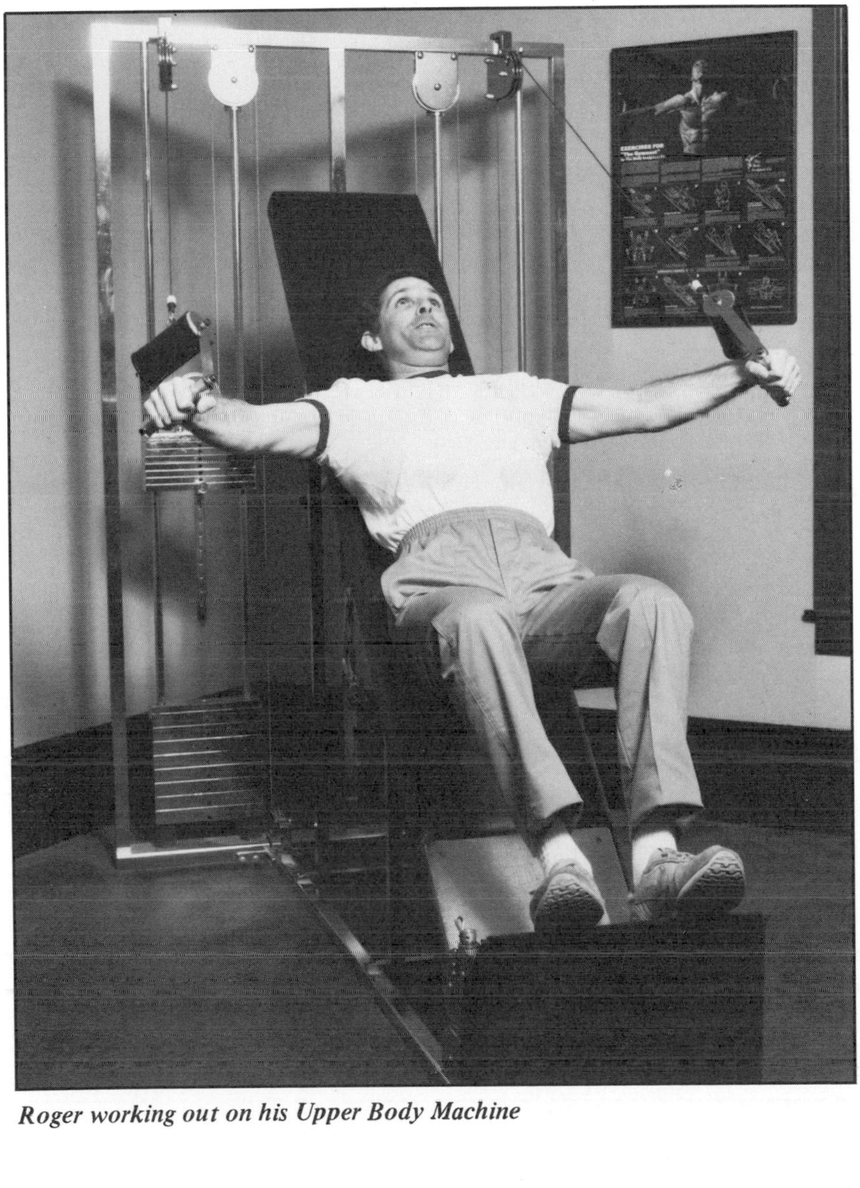

Roger working out on his Upper Body Machine

I got to Berkeley in 1964, before the Free Speech Movement. I was pretty young and naive and I figured I'd go to college and then get a job and do like everyone else. I came from a pretty conservative upper middle class Jewish area in Long Island. Suddenly here I was in Berkeley with people sitting on police cars, stormtroopers coming into the city, helicopters flying all over the place. When it became clear it wasn't the right thing to be in Vietnam, that the government was not what we'd been brought up to believe it was, we all started to look for our own answers.

People in my generation—I'm 40 now—all our values were cast away. We didn't know what to believe in, and we all found our way through the confusion in different ways. But most of us came out of it knowing we didn't want to get stuck in a structured environment.

In college, people were getting drafted if they didn't have 3.0 averages and sent to Vietnam. We were all terrified. Some people turned to drugs. A lot of my friends were on heroin and methadrine. And people did different things. I guess part of the way I asserted my individuality was to major in Norwegian. During my last 2 years, I was the only person at the University of California at Berkeley to do that. And then 3 years into medical school I took a year off to do general practice in the arctic regions of Norway.

During this year, I worked with a great general practitioner. We'd work all day and then every other night we'd make house calls, from 6 until about 1 A.M. We'd drive around the fjords, maybe 200 miles, seeing 10 or 20 people. I first worked on the west coast of Norway, then

Americans don't know moderation. If they jog, they jog too much. If they lift weights, they lift too much. Dieting is the same thing.

in the Arctic. Then I finished medical school and did a 3-year residency in family practice.

I started doing emergency room work because I didn't want to be on a 9 to 5 schedule every day. The pace in there fit more with my personality and lifestyle. I've been doing emergency stuff ever since and it's allowed me time for other projects.

What's this about a rock and roll band?

I worked at night with several other people. One time somebody brought a guitar and I said, "You know I used to play the guitar in high school. Why don't we start a band? We're here anyway." And we practiced every week.

Were you electrified?

Not at first. Then we got electric instruments but we couldn't blast away in the emergency room. I designed this electrical system where you could plug everything into an amp and out into headphones. We would play on our instruments, and the singer had a mike—we had echo chambers and everything—and we were the only people who could hear it. We wired up a little box so we could even plug in taped music into one ear of the headphones and we could play in the other ear. *(Laughter)* We did that for years at night. Then we formed a band and started playing professionally. The band is still in existence here in Petaluma. I stayed with it for about 2½ years but I'm not in it anymore.

Do you have specific ideas about diet?

People in America tend to go overboard. We accomplish a helluva lot. And when the American public decides to do something they do it! When the American public decided to jog, goddammit, everybody went out and jogged. We got some great runners out of that and the country as a whole got into great shape compared to before. But the flip side is that Americans don't know moderation. If they jog, they jog too much. If they lift weights, they lift too much. Dieting is the same thing. We all knew we had to lose fat. So whatever we did, whether we starved, whether we used the Pritikin diet or another, we lost weight. But people start to think that fat is evil or that chocolate is evil, or ice cream. When in reality none of that stuff is evil. It's all meant to be there, it's just that we have to control it. In the last few years, I've seen a lot of over-30-year-old athletes get into endurance sports. They tend to be the kind of people who can suffer through enormous amounts of pain and agony to reach a goal. For that I think they deserve an enormous amount of credit. But they also tend to take things too far. With the dieting, people have lost so much body weight that they're losing their lean body mass, they're losing their muscles, and they're turning into anorexics.

You think a lot of people are anorexic that don't know it? A lot of runners?

I think an enormous amount are. It's hard to know when to apply that definition. For example, I met a 40-year-old marathon runner on an airport bus one time. He told me that every time he ate he wrote down how many calories it was and how far he'd have to run to burn it off. He'd put on his shoes after dinner and he'd run it off. Now he didn't consider himself an anorexic but he still is consumed by that feeling of guilt when he eats and the necessity of working it off.

What's the danger point? When you start consuming body tissue?

Right. For all of us over 30, there's a chance of getting into an accident or having to go into the hospital. When you do, if you don't have any fat, you're going to burn your lean body mass. Laying around in a hospital bed, you lose a pound a day. If you don't have any fat, you're going to be losing muscle. I really have a feeling that all of us over 30 should be carrying 5 lbs. of fat.

What percentage do you think a man should be?

For men 15% seems reasonable. I don't think I'd worry if somebody was 18% but if a man gets down to 4%, I would.

You think 10% is reasonable?

Yeah. It's lean but not dangerous. But I think if a man is doing endurance activities and he's killing himself because he thinks he's eating too much and he's 10% body fat, then he's gotta re-evaluate or get some psychiatric help.

What about women?

Well, women are higher, you know. They say women can be 20%; 18% would be lean. But if a woman gets down to 10% she's probably too lean. Unless she's a world-class competitive athlete.

Somebody's gonna say, "I'm not worried about being in the hospital." Are there other disadvantages to being that low in body fat?

I think it makes us susceptible to different kinds of infections and diseases. This is not based on a scientific study. But I've seen that when people get too low in body fat they get aches and pains, more frequent colds, and they're just not as healthy as they were before. I don't know if I can back that up with anything medical. I just have a feeling after doing medicine for 10 years that there's some kind of reason for us to have body fat. It's a storage. It's an energy supply It's kind of a savings account for us. Insurance policy. If you take that away, your skin might look paper thin and that might be great when you're naked, but when you are in need of some energy supplies, you're going to need fat. It's just like the endurance athletes that need glycogen. God, if they don't have any extra stores in their body, how far can they run before they run out of steam? □

Ray Bright

Roger Minkow doing a "front lever" in 1980 with Maurice Williams, a Canadian gymnast, watching

Roger Monks

Alice Wrobley

Roger Monks, a San Francisco fireman, builds bikes, collects vintage Porsches and takes epic cycling trips: one from Vancouver, B.C. down the west coast to San Francisco (about 1200 miles), another from San Diego through Baja, California to Cabo San Lucas; and a third from San Francisco to New Orleans, some 2440 miles in 24 days.

Vital Statistics
Roger Monks, 54
Date of Birth: October 19, 1931
Born: St. Louis, Missouri
Height: 5'10½" **Weight**: 168
Job: Fireman
Lives in: San Francisco, California
Activities: Cycling

I'll never forget, when I was a kid back in St. Louis, about 11 years old, when I first saw the newspaper boy coming down the street. He had an old-fashioned track bike and his newspaper bag over his shoulder. He was going down the street freehand and throwing papers on the doorsteps while riding the bike. Like a circus act. That was really the cat's meow. The way to be.

How many miles a day did you cover on that trip to New Orleans?

I averaged about 180 miles a day. You get up at dawn. I like to get a minimum of 20 miles in before breakfast—get the system going before I eat. Then it's a good practice to digest at least a half an hour after a meal. Then, naturally, you'll stop at unexpected scenic vistas, not like when you're in an automobile and just fly by and say, "Jeez, I wish I had stopped there."

You're really on the road snacking all day—that's my habit of touring. You might stop for fresh fruit and you consume a lot of liquid so you have to stop and replenish it. On this ride we stopped in motels. I didn't carry any overnight camping equipment.

How'd you carry your gear?

Pannier bags—one over each side on the back and a handlebar bag that balances the load forward and aft. The handlebar bag is convenient to get to while you're rolling—to grab a scarf, a pair of sunglasses. The bike weighs about 23 lbs. and I carried about 25 lbs. of tools, changes of clothes, parts, essentials. So a total of about 50 lbs.

On this ride we stopped in motels. I didn't carry any overnight camping equipment.

Paul Butler

What's your rain gear?

I don't really have rain gear. Mostly you're concerned about cold wind on your chest. The old-timers used newspapers. They're good insulation. Just shove it down your shirt. I did just get a Goretex jacket and some polypropylene underwear.

Could you travel lighter than 50 lbs.?

No. That's about the minimum. A typical tourist that isn't going for long mileage might go twice that weight. Usually they carry a tent, sleeping bag, cooking gear and clothes they never use.

Did you stay on small roads?

No, I went on the interstate. Except in California where they're pretty darn strict about enforcing the law. I rode highways in Arizona and Texas even where it said "No bicycles allowed." The locals told me not to worry about it. And they were right.

How were the people you met?

I enjoyed meeting everyone. It's a lot easier to meet strangers. Especially in restaurants they were curious. When you start, you're far from your destination and they're interested that you have that ambition. Then as you get closer, they're amazed that you've come all the way from California.

When I got to New Orleans, I was introduced to the audience at a Louisiana Jazz Ensemble concert. I was introduced as "this nut who's ridden all the way from California."

Do you recommend a road bike or a mountain bike for long distance riding?

Definitely a road bike. The bike I used—an old BSA I've had since '52—was pretty much the standard in the immediate post-war years. Long wheel base for a little softer ride. A relatively stiff frame. Stiff frames transmit your physical and muscular energy more directly to the road. The more flex in the frame, the more energy you're losing in mechanical disadvantage. But you do get a softer ride. So it's a trade-off.

What should a triathlete or a bike racer look for?

Besides the stiff frame, they should think about two sets of wheels. One for training and one for racing. You should get your bike set up by a professional. Exact geometry for your physical frame. Adjust the handlebars and the saddle—those variables, besides the rigid shape of the frame itself, can make a lot of difference in a race or on a hundred-miler. □

Bill Pearl

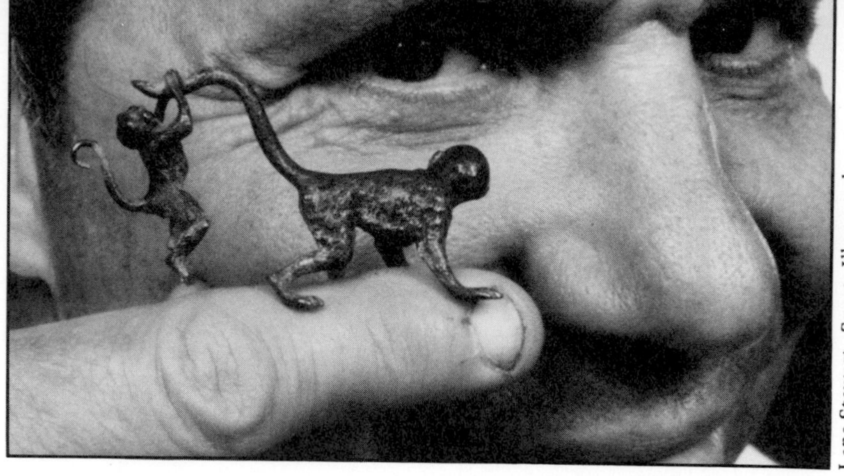

Lane Stewart–Sports Illustrated

At 3 A.M. each morning, 6 days a week, an alarm goes off in a house near Medford, Oregon. Hours before even farmers are up, Bill Pearl gets out of bed, makes himself a pot of herbal tea, and by 4 A.M. is in his gym doing what he's been doing for over 40 years–pumping iron.

Talk to almost anyone who lifted weights in the '50s and they'll invariably tell you their hero was Bill Pearl. In 1953 he accomplished the hitherto impossible, winning the Mr. California, Mr. America and Mr. Universe contests. In 1956 he won the Mr. USA contest and in 1961 and again in 1967 won the professional Mr. Universe titles. In 1971 Bill astounded the bodybuilding world by winning the Mr. Universe contest again at age 41.

Bill ran gyms in Sacramento and Los Angeles for about 25 years. In the early '80s he compiled what soon became the definitive text on weight training: a remarkable 638 page book, with 1500 different exercises called Keys to the Inner Universe–The Encyclopedia of Weight Training. *The book contains some 3000 drawings of exercises, as well as chapters on Bill's career, philosophy, and advice on diet, physiology, steroids and training for contests. It was sold by mail order and in weightlifting stores (not in bookstores) for $32.95. In 4 years it sold over 50,000 copies.*

One day I picked up the phone and called Bill at his office in Oregon. Would he be interested in doing a smaller version at a lower price available to the public in bookstores? He liked the idea immediately and in ensuing months we began sketching out the idea for a new and different book. We're now about halfway through preparation of Getting Stronger, *which will include weight training in general as well as specific exercises for each of 17 sports.*

In a feature article in Sports Illustrated *in 1983, writer Terry Todd called Bill "... the Sam Snead, Bill Tilden, George Blanda, Gordie Howe of bodybuilding." Todd has an interesting theory: that progressive resistance weight training may stimulate extra production of the male hormone testosterone whereas (due to stress) endurance exercises like running, swimming or cycling do not. If you think about it, veteran weightlifters, including Bill, do look surprisingly youthful.*

Bill is a Nez Perce Indian and grew up in Yakima, Washington. He started training when he was 12. In 1950, while in the Navy, he met Leo Stern, a weightlifter and gym owner in San Diego, California. Leo agreed to coach Bill. Three years later Bill won his unprecedented triple contest crowns.

Today, Bill has the same effect on people as he did 30 years ago. People come up to him in restaurants, at colleges, in the street–just to talk or shake his hand. He always takes the time to say something encouraging. Even kids aren't immune: our 5-year-old saw Bill's book sitting around and was fascinated. He started talking about Bill Pearl and how he was going to be strong like that when he grew up. His younger brother, age 3, caught the spirit. Soon milk, potatoes and previously untouched vegetables were being consumed in our household because "I'm going to get strong like Bill Pearl." The first time I brought Bill out to our home, the boys waited up, thrilled. When we were late arriving, the boys, unbeknownst to their mother, snuck out of the house in pajamas with a flashlight and walked a block down the gravel road to await our arrival. When we finally did arrive they ran over to him and wanted him to feel their muscles.

Vital Statistics
Bill Pearl, 55
Date of Birth: October 31, 1930
Born: Prinesville, Oregon
Height: 5'10½" **Weight:** 230
Job: Owner, Bill Pearl Enterprises
Lives in: Medford, Oregon
Activities: Bodybuilding

I started trying to improve myself when I was about 12 years old. I'd do push-ups, sit-ups and lift things. Dynamic Tension too.

Did you know about Charles Atlas then?

Yes, but I could never afford his courses. But I knew there had to be a way to get bigger and stronger. I had an older brother who was continually pounding on me and I think he did more to spur me on than anybody. *(Laughter)*

I have some eggs in my diet and some low-fat cottage cheese and other cheese, yes. But I don't eat any animal flesh.

How important was Leo Stern to you?

If it wasn't for Leo I'd never have competed. He spurred me on and encouraged me. What Leo aimed for, and a lot of people are missing these days, is symmetry. He wanted balance, an overall harmony. He made you work on your weaknesses.

How important is the mental aspect of training? Like if you're working on your biceps, do you do any visualization?

I don't visualize specifically my biceps, but I visualize the overall results. That I'm on stage, picked the winner. And another thing, I would never get up to 250 lbs. and trim down to 195 like everybody does today. I'd get pretty light in my body weight. Then I'd say, "I'm going to enter the contest weighing 240 or 242 lbs." I was more concerned with getting as much muscle mass as I possibly could, just before the contest.

What happens when lifters get heavy and then cut back?

It makes them very, very lean and very, very muscular but they don't have any muscular size. They look gaunt. And that's what's selling today in hardcore bodybuilding, not muscle mass.

What has the trend been lately?

To more of a small, skinny, Frank Zane-type physique. Chris Dickerson, Muhammad McCalley, those people are quite small. Very symmetrical. Have a lot of hardcore muscularity, but are not big, heavy, thick-muscled men. You could put them in street clothes and you would hardly realize they trained.

You've trained a lot of people too. How many?

Not counting myself, I've trained 8 Mr. America winners, and 10 Mr. Universe winners.

Why do you think people lift? Is it different for bodybuilders?

I still think that anybody who's heavy into weightlifting, power lifting, or bodybuilding has a tremendous amount of insecurity. A lot of these kids from smaller countries, where the economy is quite poor, not only train for perhaps an ego problem, but it's a way for them, if they can hit it big, to raise their standard of living. If a person can set goals and achieve them, it will relate to other aspects of his lifestyle. He can become a better person. If he can concentrate on this, he can do it on the job—banking, medicine, whatever.

What changes have you seen since the '50s?

More people now recognize weight training and bodybuilding as sport, as a way of keeping physically fit. People used to think you were either homosexual or you were all brawn and no brains.

What caused things to change?

The coaches started putting multi-purpose gyms in schools, and it improved kids' athletic ability, their grades came up, their self-image improved. And then the physique contests and people such as Schwarzenegger—give the guy credit, he did a lot for the sport. Maybe most important, coaches of *all* sports began to realize that their athletes could improve performance, whether it was a defensive tackle or a tennis player, by weight training. They finally got around the myth of being muscle-bound. And of course women getting involved has had a tremendous impact. The darn sport evolved from the basement to the backyard to what it is today. It's been an evolution.

Say somebody comes into your gym and they don't want to do bodybuilding, but they want to get stronger and faster in swimming or skiing or cycling. What do you tell them?

First, even if this guy is in shape, he's not conditioned to lift weights. It's a different ballgame. So, I will put him on a general training program, even if he is a world-class skier. After an initial program of maybe a month or two I'd start getting specific. Like I wouldn't give him a 500 lb. squat. He doesn't need this to ski down a hill. He can do non-lock squats, where he doesn't come up to a full extension of the knee, because he's usually riding and never ever locking his legs out. Simulate the movement he's going to be making on the hill. And a lot of oblique work at twisting. And strength development of the shoulders and the arms. We'd also work the forearms because you need forearm strength for working the poles. Wrists too.

For a long distance swimmer, high repetitions with relatively low weight would give you sinewy and hard muscle. The body will condition itself for long-distance endurance. But if we get a sprinter, a track person where there's just a short burst, the faster he can propel or the quicker he can pull a leg up in the air, the faster he can run. So he does exercises to improve his burst of speed. Like jump squats, where

Leo Stern

1967 Mr. Universe

Leo Stern

1971 Mr. Universe

you go down and jump up high like a basketball player. Do it with weights. And again, you just don't have to use heavy, heavy poundage for that.

Now, in football, where you just gotta move this guy out of the road one time and then come back 3 minutes later and move him out again . . . that's when your 500-lb. squats and 400-lb. bench presses come into play. That's hardcore strengthening. You've got to adapt any particular training program to the particular sport.

What's your current idea on diet? You used to eat meat. Then what happened?

Twenty years ago my joints were sore and stiff. It felt like arthritis. My cholesterol was 247. Then Judy and I gave up red meat and were eating chicken and fish. Then, we'd be eating chicken and crack it open and there'd be a great big growth on the joints . . . the female hormones they feed them. I certainly didn't want those floating around in my system. I wanted to be a big old husky jock. So I stopped eating chicken. Then this mercury scare came along, so I threw the fish out. So here I am today.

Do you eat dairy products?

I have some eggs in my diet and some low-fat cottage cheese and other cheese, yes. But I don't eat any animal flesh. And I never make substitutions or say, "Hey, lookit. I'm on the road and things are tough." I just don't do it.

You never get a burger?

No, never. I'll either fast or wait until I can find something.

And you haven't felt any less energy from doing this?

No, I probably have more energy. But I'm much more tranquil. I'm a kinder person and I used to be a real hard ass. If anybody even wanted to think about giving me any trouble I was just thrilled to death.

Do you think you got that hard edge from eating meat?

Part of it was certainly being raised in an area where you had to prove yourself. And because of being Indian . . . I was pushed around as a third-class citizen. Even though I felt I was a nice person—if anybody even pushed me or commenced to challenge me in any way—I was ready to go at it. But since I married Judy and changed my eating habits, my life has definitely changed.

What does your workout consist of these days?

I still train 6 days a week, 2½-3 hours a day. And the only time that changes is when I'm training for a physique contest or an exhibition. Then I just spend more time on my posing, more time on my eating habits. I'm in the gym at ten to 4 and I train until 7-7:30 every morning.

Bill, 55, guest posing at Derby, England in 1985

I still train 6 days a week 2½–3 hours a day.

Do you try to keep your pulse up by moving fast from one exercise to another?

I keep my pulse at about 130 for 45 minutes to an hour at a time. If you handle a real heavy weight for 8 repetitions, you really tax yourself, you get your lungs working like hell. If you go jump to something else and you do 8 more, and your body still hasn't recovered, your blood will be pumping because that oxygen is racing in there to get your muscles to recover from the previous workload.

So that's one way to improve your cardiovascular while you're lifting weights.

No doubt about it. Now if you rest in between exercises, you get zero cardiovascular benefit. But a trained bodybuilder who keeps things moving, keeps that pulse up, will get a great aerobic workout just in the gym.

Why did you decide to get out of competitive bodybuilding?

I had been prodded and pushed by magazines for years to compete against Schwarzenegger and any new face that came on. I was like Muhammad Ali, the guy everybody had to knock off. This went on for nearly 20 years. And you get sick of it. You walk around and say, "Jesus, is this really me?" You're like the prime pig everywhere you go. I couldn't live my own life. So I figured, "Hey, look, I'm still going to weight train but I'm going to take up cycling and pull my weight down and get in condition where everybody in the industry realizes I'm not a threat to anybody!" So I rode bikes and I got my weight down to 185. I told 'em, "Go hassle Arnold; don't hassle me anymore."

How did you feel when you weighed 185?

Horrible. Psychologically I felt bad.

Were you dieting then?

Yeah. I'd fast for 7 days at a time. And I lost a tremendous amount of muscle mass. I wasn't happy with myself. When I came back and started training again I discovered the cycling was much more detrimental to my bodybuilding than I had imagined. It took a long time for my strength to come back. Heavy squats and heavy benching were almost impossible.

How long did it take you to build back?

Maybe a year and a half, 2 years. And my legs weren't stronger and in better condition—they were better conditioned for endurance but not on the weights.

Now you're going to be doing what you're doing for the rest of your life probably.

I hope so. Unless something happens, I'll train from here on out. □

Judy Pearl

Judy Pearl and her husband Bill share their splendidly equipped home gym for 2½-3 hours of weight training six mornings a week. Judy is also responsible for the lacto-ovo-vegetarian dishes that keep these high-powered athletes fortified. As a former gym owner, Judy has had many opportunities to witness the physical and psychological benefits of weight training for women.

Susan was my best friend in high school and when we graduated and no longer had the school P.E. classes, we started noticing we were losing muscle tone and gaining weight. My dad had exercised a lot—he was a Bernarr MacFadden follower. I was sort of raised on blackstrap molasses and yogurt. So I started calling around and ended up joining a gym in North Hollywood. I was 19.

I started working out immediately. Susan eloped and never started. Then the gal that was the instructor at the gym got a job dancing in Las Vegas. So the owner asked me if I'd like to start managing the women's exercises. I had worked there a little bit part time before then. He was getting tired of the business, plus he owed me a lot of back wages. So I just ended up buying him out and taking over his obligations.

Vital Statistics
Judy Pearl, 43
Date of Birth: February 20, 1943
Born: Los Angeles, California
Height: 5'8" **Weight**: 138
Job: Bookkeeper
Lives in: Medford, Oregon
Activities: Bodybuilding

Do you have any favorite stories about people improving themselves in your gym?

One of my favorite people is a woman who'd been paraplegic for 10 years. She called me up one day and asked if we had a bicycle in the gym and if we could help her try to make a revolution on the pedals. So she came in and we had to strap her feet to the pedals because she had no control of her legs or feet. And she really worked with us and finally got the pedal to go around one half a turn, then a full turn. She was elated. The next time she made it go around 15 times. The next time, 45 times. We had to lift her off and on things but she could do a lot of pulley work. If we set just the right weight on the pulley it would lift her leg up and she would work and get it to come back down. She had little bits of muscle impulses to certain parts of her legs that she hadn't used because she didn't know it was possible. She got to where she could do sit-ups by having a pulley with a weight stack helping her up. So she worked her back and abdominals. She worked her legs and hips from different areas. And because of the bicycle she got to where she was walking with Canadian crutches by the time it was all over. And it was just through weight training—the use of pulleys and the bicycle and determination.

Another gal who came to the gym had had polio. She had a real old lady image. She wore her long hair in a big bun. She wore black all the time and flat heel shoes. No makeup. She looked really old for her age. She had a daughter who was in her late teens and they were good friends. They came in and worked out together. The mother couldn't get up off the floor by herself without help when she started. We got her doing sit-ups with the help of a pulley, and she strengthened her hip girdle muscles and legs. Did leg extensions and things. She got to where not only could she get up by herself, she went on a white water river trip a few years after she started at the gym. She came in and told me how much the gym had turned her life around. She practically made me cry. She could wear high heel shoes now because she had more strength. She got a younger hair style and started dressing brighter. Her whole attitude was totally different because she was able to do things through exercise that no doctors or therapists had been able to help her with.

I just hate to see young people come into the gym and think something is too hard for them. If you're 24 years old and it's too difficult for you to do now and it makes you puff and sweat, where are you going to be by the time you're 30?

You feel that working out and improving your looks go hand in hand?

Oh, yeah. Anybody that sticks with it. You don't necessarily end up looking like Raquel Welch or Rachel McLish, but working out improves your self image and mental attitude; you have more energy. We had a lady who was an alcoholic and had had a nervous breakdown. She slept 15 or more hours a day. And her husband brought her in to see us. She had to be coaxed, so every excuse she came up with, I'd counter with why she

Like a wild animal, a cat, when you can see the outlines of its muscularity, it's a live, graceful kind of thing.

Lane Stewart—Sports Illustrated

should just try it. Gosh, she was just a totally different person. Turned her whole life around—hers and his. Where before she'd been sleeping all the time and staying in the house, overweight and crying, now she'd be the first person at the gym every morning. She took on babysitting jobs. She just became a happier person. These kinds of transformations are so commonplace that I don't even think about it.

What's your workout these days?

I do exactly what Bill does. But I don't work forearms and neck. I work as long as he does except for about 20 minutes (2½-3 hours).

Do you do roughly the same type of exercises he does but just with less weight?

Yes. We work back and legs and abs on Monday, biceps and triceps on Tuesday, and deltoids and chest on Wednesday. Thursday we start back with legs and back. We work chest and back, legs and shoulders. Those are what we work together. We work different body parts on the different days.

Do you see something different going on with women now than there was 10 years ago?

For years there have been more women attending gyms and exercising than men. But it's just recently that women have felt that it's all right for their muscles to show. And to have a lean, muscular appearance, be proud of having the curves that come from their muscle structure instead of thinking they have to look like Playboy bunnies. Possibly the women's movement had a little bit to do with that. The truth is, it doesn't matter if a woman has big breasts or not, it's how she feels about herself. Like a wild animal, a cat, when you can see the outlines of its muscularity it's a live, graceful kind of thing. □

Trudy Renggli

Trudy Renggli has a contagious good nature, an absolutely democratic approach to people, and a surprising lack of vanity. Ask her what sports she participates in, the kind of work she does, even what language she speaks and it will be hard for her to answer briefly. She loves any sport– "As long as I move I don't really care what I'm doing."–has lived in 3 different countries, and speaks five languages: French, German, Italian, English and some Spanish.

Trudy grew up in Switzerland, went to school in a French-speaking region, then went to England to learn English. There, she worked as a governess, then took a job in the Italian part of Switzerland, learned Italian, did a lot of mountaineering and played tennis competitively. "Itchy for travel," Trudy was an air hostess for Swissair for three years, and also worked for the Circle of Art who made reproductions of great paintings.

These days Trudy lives in Bolinas, California, and works for Shelter Publications. At home, she works at book restoration and binding, and sells potato print greeting cards made with organic home-grown potatoes from her garden. She does not consciously schedule sports into her week: "I don't think I've missed many days without at least walking or bicycling... My body always seems to feel like doing something, whether it is chopping wood or working in the garden, playing tennis, swimming, or going for a walk with my two dogs. When I move my body feels great and my heart laughs."

–Marianne Orina

Vital Statistics

Trudy Renggli, 56
Date of Birth: August 7, 1929
Born: Lucerne, Switzerland
Height: 5'4" **Weight**: 130
Job: Secretary, typesetter
Lives in: Bolinas, California
Activities: Walking, hiking, kayaking, swimming, tennis, Tai-Chi, horseback riding

You seem to be a very balanced, level headed and optimistic person. What do you attribute it to?

Mostly to love of life and to exercise.

Does it have anything to do with being Swiss and loving chocolate? *(Laughter)*

Well, a piece of chocolate now and then does help to enjoy life.

Were you active as a child?

When I was a child in Switzerland, we didn't have a car, we either walked or bicycled to school. In order to get somewhere you just had to use your legs or your bike, otherwise you were stuck.

In terms of sports, do you feel like little girls were encouraged to be as active as little boys?

I was very active as a girl but I was considered a tomboy. I actually did not like to play handball with girls because they never threw it as hard. When I threw it they all disappeared. So I always played with boys. All sports.

Did your parents buy you skis at an early age?

Oh no. We lived in a house with a big sloping courtyard in back. I used to see the neighborhood kids skiing down those tiny slopes in the back. I was dying to go skiing. I was about 5 or 6 and my dad couldn't afford to buy me a pair of skis that Christmas. We had all kinds of wonderful wooden spoons hanging on the wall over the stove. I took two of them and told my mother to strap them to my feet. She couldn't figure out what on earth I was going to do and I said, well, I want a pair of skis. So she said, oh well, it cannot do any harm and strapped those spoons to my little boots. I went out to the hill and to have two wooden spoons on my feet gave me the feeling of having a pair of skis. That was actually my first skiing experience. After that my father could not resist and he did buy me a pair of skis.

Then you would ski in the mountains?

We would take our skis, tie them to the side of our bike, bike 5 miles to the mountain, then walk up to the top of the hill with seal furs strapped to the bottom.

Seal furs?

You strapped them on the skis so you didn't slide back; the short fur feels like stroking a cat the wrong way, it gives resistance and holds you on the slope. You could walk up steep hills. When we arrived at the top of the mountain we would take them off, let them dry in the sun while we had a bite to eat out of the rucksack and then strap them around our waists and ski down again.

So all that was for one glorious slide?

Yes, it took so long to get there, to walk up, have lunch on top, sit in the sun and ski down.

That sounds nice.

It was beautiful. There were no ski-lifts. And if you were the first ones

1951, Chiasso, Switzerland

In 1950 with friend's airplane, Agno, Switzerland

1949, Southwold, England

1949, Southwold, England

Marcia Miner

1983, Stinson Beach, California

1949, Southwold, England

Jack Fulton

down it was satisfying to make the first traces in the snow, sometimes next to a pawprint of some wild animal.

I have a list of all the sports you participate in now. Tennis, Tai-Chi, swimming, hiking, kayaking, table-tennis, horseback riding, boules, gardening and skiing. Do you still ski?

Oh yes, whenever I get a chance. Every winter when I see snow on television I get a little homesick for the mountains. When it is sunny and dry like it is in California, I think tennis instead. You have to smell the snow, that's when it gets you all excited. Just like the smell of food stimulates your appetite.

You seem to choose sports that have a certain type of pace and rhythm.

Basically I don't like speed. Never did. I mean even when I ski, I don't like to schuss, I like to slalom, and Tai-Chi I like because it has a slow rhythm. Tennis you can make slow or fast depending on the partner. I wouldn't like running because I love to hike and walk. You see things on the way and if I saw a flower I had never seen before, running by it and not stopping to look at it would be very hard for me.

The pace in our society is so fast now; you seem to move with the pace of nature, maybe the seasons.

I like that rhythm and actually in sports like tennis I very often count. Like, one when the partner hits the ball, two when it hits the ground and three when I hit it. Especially at the beginning in order to get into a certain rhythm. When I get going too fast, I get an uneasy feeling. I don't handle pressure very well. I can work very long hours but it has to be at a certain rhythm. The minute I am pressured I lose my balance completely and start spinning, going round in circles and nothing, nothing gives. That's where Tai-Chi works like a miracle drug. Fifteen minutes of it and I'm back to normal.

Was there any point during your life when you felt like you didn't have time to exercise?

No, it was always part of my life. I get very irritated when I don't move. I feel this kind of mental irritation when I'm locked into a room.

When you first came to the United States was it just for a tourist visit or were you thinking of living here?

I was flying for Swissair at that time, and I met an American and her mother who invited me to visit them

in San Francisco. When I did, I fell in love with the city and stayed for 11 years.

Didn't you work in a Swiss bank for a while?

Yes, I had returned to Switzerland because my mother got very sick. I was working as an officer in a bank in Geneva. I worked in portfolio management and had clients from all over the world. They usually came with a pile of money and said: "I'll be back next year, do what you can." Depending on whether they were gamblers or starchy conservative investors, you had to invest accordingly. It was challenging. It got to a point where the market got so crazy that when you came into the office in the morning with a fixed investment idea, two hours later everything was topsy-turvy. Somewhere in the world a catastrophe happened, a threat of war, a silver king that tried to corner the market, etc., etc., and the market plunged. The pressure built up, the pace got more and more frantic and finally it was pure gambling. It's hard to gamble with someone else's money. You want to show them profit, you don't like to lose. It's easier to lose your own money.

Maybe.

So anyway my mother got sick and I started thinking, gee, what am I doing all this for, earning a lot of money and not really having a lot of time on this 8 hour job. Most people had an 8 hour job and what did they do? They had 3-4 weeks holiday per year, traveled to far-away places in search of sunshine and warmth and were more tired when they came back than when they started. So I thought, I've got to change something in my life. To make a long story short, I went on a hike up the mountain, rested on a bench under a tree. A bird was sitting on a branch, happily singing away. Trudy, I said, you don't know the name of the tree, you don't know the name of the bird, all you know is how to juggle with figures, gold, silver and pork bellies. This is absurd. I got a shot of adrenaline that lasted all night long. The next day I called the bank and gave them my resignation. First I slowed down to 3 days per week and finally said goodbye to the world of money. The horizon was shining more brightly than any gold coin. □

Amleto Rossi

Amleto Rossi grew up on the outskirts of Rome during the second World War. Food was scarce, but the quality was good, he recalls, since people took the time to prepare it well. Amleto worked at many trades in Rome: plumber, painter, construction worker, dental technician and finally owner of an antique shop. In 1965 he married an American and came to New York, where he went to work at the New York Times.

After several years in New York he began to get allergies from the dust in subways and headed west with his wife and two children. He got a job in Los Angeles working on a movie. The producer died unexpectedly just before the movie was completed, the money ran out and Amleto headed north to Bolinas, just north of San Francisco, to visit a friend. He never went back.

About ten years ago Amleto made some pizza for a local celebration. People started asking him to make more and he now makes take-out pizza six nights a week in his home. It's not Pizza Hut pizza, but rather the stuff Italian mamas make, hand kneaded, individually prepared, made to order.

Vital Statistics
Amleto Rossi, 49
Date of Birth: August 24, 1936
Born: Rome, Italy
Height: 5'8" **Weight**: 140
Job: Pizza maker
Lives in: Bolinas, California
Activities: Tennis, cycling, soccer

You know . . . eating is like a habit, an addiction. Especially the way food is now. The more you eat, the more you want. It's self-perpetuating. Food is a stimulant. Especially with all this prepared food these days. That's why there are so many overweight people. Prepared food, canned food and frozen food have a lot of chemicals. A lot of sweeteners. A lot of salt. Once you start tasting the food, you keep on eating because the taste buds go berserk.

You grew up in Italy during WWII. Were you hungry?

We'd go in the fields and get fruit and vegetables. There were little farms. We could go there and even steal chickens. You have no morals when you are hungry. You don't feel you are doing anything criminal. Now we are confused about eating because there is not that absolute need to sustain yourself. You don't know if you are eating because you're hungry or because you are triggered. The system doesn't know what to do.

What do you eat?

I don't worry about it at all. Something about my metabolism. I've been the same size since I became a man. I never had to diet in my life. In a week, I'll have fish one day, maybe two days a week some meat. A lot of soup. And bread is wonderful. I make my own bread. I feel very fulfilled. Bread and pasta—it is a wonderful food because it's satisfying, easy to digest and easy to make. My boys want the pizza of course, but I have it maybe once a week.

How do you stay in such great shape?

I don't do anything religiously. But I like to do things with my boys. I play soccer every weekend. You

Mark Fraser

Amleto in 1985

Amleto in 1969 with John Lewis of the Modern Jazz Quartet. M.J.Q. did sound track for movie Amleto was working on.

Ted Gershuny

Bread and pasta . . . it is wonderful food because it's satisfying, easy to digest and easy to make.

Jack Fulton

Jack Fulton

don't have to have a certain physical dimension to play soccer. Anybody can do it. You just have to be coordinated and able to run. There's no substitutions and no time-outs. It's exciting.

I also ride the bicycle and hit the speedbag. I have the bag right on the porch. When I come out of the house, pum, pum, pum. And tennis, too. The public court is right outside my house. I love tennis. You don't get hurt, it's clean, there's physical activity, good coordination. Just a beautiful sport.

Why did you come to America?

I came in 1965 because I married an American girl.

What did you do at the *New York Times?*

I was a Xerox machine operator. The machines were not so sophisticated then. It was ironic because I'm working for the *Times* and I don't speak any English. Not only that but I was on the same floor as all the big wheels. The people liked me and took me under their wing. They offered me a permanent spot if I'd commit to stay for 5 or 6 years. But I didn't like to live in New York. I lived in Brooklyn and took two subways to work. I got lost so many times. Once I thought I was in another country and said, "Where in the hell am I?" Plus, I couldn't stand to be on the subway 'cause I was used to fresh air. I got allergies because of all the dust.

How'd you get out to California?

After spending a year in New York, I said, "This is not America." So I came to California and it was wonderful. I arrived in January and it was sunshine and clean, manicured. My neighbor was a movie producer and he gave me a job as his assistant. I was the perfect choice because the movie was shot in Italy and he needed a liaison between the Italian and American crew. It was a great experience. But I had enough of big cities. I had to move away, to a smaller place where the air was clean, where I could breathe, where my boys could breathe. So here I am.

You seem pretty happy. What is your secret?

No secret. But every day, usually after I make the dough, I have a cup of coffee and then I like to have a couple of hours with nothing to do. I don't even answer the phone during that time because I need those couple of hours. I can get into the spectrum of things that happen. I like that part. You can do that around here because it's such a small town. □

Walt Stack

Vital Statistics

Walt Stack, 78
Date of Birth: September 29, 1907
Born: Detroit, Michigan
Height: 5'10" **Weight**: 175
Job: Retired hod carrier, seaman
Lives in: San Francisco, California
Activities: Running, swimming, cycling

Every morning during commute hours, rain or shine, you see him shuffling across the Golden Gate Bridge: a young old barrel-chested man with tattooed arms, brown as a berry, clad only in running shorts and shoes. Motorists honk, wave, yell "Hi Walt." He's as sure to be there as is the toll collector at the booth.

Ex-merchant marine, hod carrier, union organizer, Walt started running at age 58, over 20 years ago. By now he's run well over 100 marathons, including the Pike's Peak Marathon 13 times, fourteen 50-milers and three 100-mile races. He's run a marathon in 3:25, a 50-miler in 7:15 and the 100 in 17 hours. But Walt doesn't consider speed of the essence. "Start slowly and taper off," he says. In addition to running, Walt has competed in the Ride and Tie race (40 miles, one horse, two humans), has swum from the Golden Gate and Alcatraz to San Francisco several times (1-1/16 miles, 50-55° water) and completed the Ironman Triathlon in Hawaii.

On his 75th birthday in 1982, 3000 runners ("in various stages of sobriety" according to City Sports *magazine) turned out to honor Walt. Walt's no teetotaler himself. He has*

Walt running the Greek Marathon in 1977, from Marathon to Athens

an unusual ability to consume alcohol while running: 3 six-packs during a 50-mile race in Hawaii, boilermakers on a 100-mile run, and detours to two taverns along the route of the Greek Marathon.

He's had a book written about him: The Running Saga of Walt Stack *by Bob Bishop. He's been on the Johnny Carson show (probably giving the censor a nervous breakdown), is on the S.F. Mayor's Physical Fitness Council, is an active member of the AFL-CIO committee on Political Education and has appeared on an NBC sports show with Bruce Jenner. He's been a major force in promoting running programs for older people, kids and the handicapped and feels that his most important contribution has been his promotion of equal rights for women in sports.*

I first came to San Francisco in about 1926. I was going to sea and the first time I docked here I liked it. Then when the '34 maritime strike happened I was asked to come out to Seattle. The left wing had its union there and they wanted me to take it over because the crazy bastard that was running it, got too much pleasure out of how much blood he got out of the end of a club beating on scabs. So I was up there a few years. Then I came down the coast and I've been here ever since. Got married and spent less and less time at sea and more and more time ashore.

You were a hod carrier. Was that pretty heavy work?

I could carry up to 150 lbs., but I'd be goddamned if I would. I'd carry about 100, enough to keep the boss from saying, "Hey for Christsakes, what's the matter here?"

Then I run across the bridge to Sausalito and back, about 17 miles. Then another swim and bike back home.

What made you start running?

I took it up to improve my lung power for competitive swimming. I'd swum for years, in tropical waters all over the world. It wasn't a fine technique or nothin'. Just a slob in the water but I had fun. I swam good enough to do the Ironman and that's a 2½ mile swim. (*Along with a 26-mile run and 118-mile bike ride*).

When was that?

In '81. But the water was kind of turbulent and if I'd swum my usual style with my head above water I'd have swallowed half the ocean. So I swam side stroke and breast stroke. It took me 4½ hours.

You know, when I first started swimming in the Bay here, someone asked me, "How long can you swim?" I says, "Shit, all day I guess." I didn't realize how different it was around here from tropical waters. See, in real warm water you don't get tired. But here, even in the middle of the summer, you can last only so long. It's cold and it takes all your strength.

How cold is it in winter in S.F. Bay?

About 48-50°. You really have to be motivated to get your ass out there in this cold water. See, you're swimming here and then when you come in you reach up here *(grabs his throat)* and say, "Jesus Christ, have I got a goiter?" It's just your balls up there, you know? *(Laughter)*

What do you do these days to keep in shape?

Each day I ride my bike over to the club (Dolphins Club on S.F. Bay). It takes about an hour. Then I take a little swim. Then I run across the bridge to Sausalito and back, about 17 miles. Then another swim and bike back home. I do that five days a week. Saturdays and Sundays I take off and help clean up the house.

Have you had many injuries?

Well, I broke a few ribs riding my

Walt Stack on his daily run, a round trip to Sausalito from San Francisco

bike. Hit the railroad tracks wrong one day. And heel spurs and stress fractures from the running, but that's about all.

I guess you've figured out how much you can do.

Oh yeah. I've slowed down a lot. There's a general degeneration of the body at a certain age. But you know, I know quite a few runners—now they're in their 50s, not 70s—who are as good now as when they were in college.

What's the story I hear about you being in Alcatraz?

I was a prisoner there. At the time (1925), it was a military prison. I was in for desertion and fraudulent enlistment. See, I joined the Army when I was only 15. Lied about my age. And after about a year of that shit . . . my attention span wasn't up to it, so I took off. But after about 9 months I decided that maybe when I grew up I might want to get a federal job and with that on my record, Jesus, it looked like hell. So I got back in the Army under an assumed name. Everything went well until they sent me to the Philippines. It was the rainy season and I got fed up so I told them I was a deserter and all that. I got sentenced to 18 months.

What was it like out there? *(We were sitting on a bench by the bay, looking out at Alcatraz.)*

Well, it was really rough because the biggest single problem a young man would have, I was 17 then, is all these wolves that got tired of Madame Thumb and her 4 daughters and they wanted to, you know . . . So you're either fighting off these bastards or you're becoming a punk. I made up my mind and passed the word around—some of these people rapin' somebody, some had even been caught 4 or 5 times and got 5 years added each time but it didn't mean anything to them. I was on the rock pile. I had bars and rocks and different things layin' around all over the place. I said, "I'm going to kill the first cocksucker that makes a pass at me." You couldn't tell the officials,

I was a left-winger, you know. It's a euphemism for a progressive, left-wing activist.

you know, because then you're a rat. And they can step out of a line and cut you up or kill you. You have no choice. You either gotta be a stool pigeon—what they call a rat—or you give in, or you fight. So I made up my mind to fight. That was the most scary part of my life. I got off the rock pile and they put me in the laundry. It was more controlled and less likelihood of something like that happening. But it was a terrible thing. Just imagine being faced with that . . . I imagine a woman feels the same way. The thought of being raped . . . .

You were active in the union for a while.

I was a business agent for 10 years. Marine Fireman's Union—the engine department on ships. I always got the biggest vote of anybody in spite of having the handicap, if you want to put it that way, of being known as a communist. I never made any bones about it. I am and I was for over 50 years. Tough to be at all popular when you got people red-baitin' you—the McCarthy period and all that stuff. Even in strike cases where I got pinched or something, some prosecuting attorney would get up, "This man is a deserter from the U.S. Army." I had to tell them I was just a shit-ass kid, didn't know any better, there was no great harm done and all that to nullify that point. Desertion in those days wasn't a big deal. There were 70-80,000 people, which was the whole American Army practically, turning over every year.

I read an article that described you as a populist. What does that refer to?

That's just another way of sayin' I was a left-winger, you know. It's a euphemism for progressive, left-wing, activist.

What was going on in the McCarthy years for you? Was it a stressful time?

I got followed around by the FBI and had them ease me off jobs and shit like that. I was on one job and I see a man comin' along and he's got a squad of soldiers and a rifle. Navy men, you know. They come and ask, "Mr. Stack here?" "Yeah, he's over there." "Well, he can't work here." No argument. No reason. Just "Get off." That kind of shit where you're on the job and they pass the word, "Red." So in that period, even if you weren't red, but were associated with a red you were in trouble. In fact, it hit some people so badly they committed suicide. Especially people who didn't know communism from rheumatism and then got held up as reds. It was terrible.

What does it mean being in the communist party?

Well, it depends on who you're talking to. If you were down among the fundamentalists in Arkansas, it would symbolize social degradation. You'd be an anti-Christ, a criminal, practically a child molester. You'd be just about everything bad. Out here it's not such a big deal, but just the same most people stay in the closet anyway. But I've never been a closet man. I figure if anybody doesn't like it, fuck 'em! *(Laughter)*

Later, I mentioned seeing Walt at the Dipsea Run breakfast the previous summer.

I can't remember the breakfast. Of course, that's an aging thing, you know. Lately, I've been thinking that as you get older, you've got so many facts in your head that there's not room for much more. Maybe it's not our brains deteriorating so much as running out of room. Well, that's probably rationalization. *(Laughter)* You've read some of Simone de Beauvoir's books, haven't you?

Not lately.

No? Well, I can speak freely then. She's an outstanding French writer. A socialist. She's in the cabinet of Mitterand, I think. And she wrote a book called *The Second Sex,* which describes some of the differences between men and women. And I can remember only one single thing of all that she said. Which is, that one of the basic reasons for marital friction between man and wife is the difference in the upbringing of the male and female child. To cite just a couple of examples: a woman is brought up to be very gentle with a major emphasis on the cosmetic approach to things. They're trained to be gentle, to be conscious of the aesthetics of things. The point I'm trying to make here is that, of all the things in the book—all of them important and interesting—the only thing I remember is this one little thing. Which shows what happens to the memory as you grow older. I have convinced myself that the reason I don't remember is because I don't need to. So I don't clutter up the mind, which would result in movin' out some stuff that I do need to know. See, that's a rationalization. □

Leo Stern

Leo Stern is a trainer of champions. Manager and owner of a gym in San Diego, California, since 1946, Leo has trained 6 Mr. Americas, including Clancy Ross and Bill Pearl, and 4 Mr. Universes. In 1942, while teaching weight training in the U.S. Air Force, Leo initiated a program of what is now called circuit training. In the '50s, in what may have been the first use of weights by a football team, he instructed the St. Augustine high school football players (San Diego) in weight training. "All we did was get them bigger and stronger." They had an undefeated season.

Left to right: Leo Stern, Dr. Craig Whitehead, J. Paul Getty and Bill Pearl at Getty's home in England, 1967. Getty was a bodybuilding fan.

What is it about your training that produces champions?

First you attempt to correct all weaknesses in a physique. We always try to get symmetry and balance to the physique, then size, and, of course, a pleasing appearance. And then the ability to pose.

In the photos of Clancy Ross and Bill Pearl you *do* see that symmetry and balance.

Both men handled heavy weights and built muscle mass and density, not just the pump. See, you can pump a lot of blood into the muscle using very light weights. But that doesn't have the long-term effect of increasing the quality and density of the muscle, the fiber, as does heavy exercise.

What about the mental aspect of training?

We always try to get the guys to concentrate deeply on each exercise. Think of the muscle and its function. Like if you're working the bicep or the tricep, think solely about that muscle and you'll get the maximum effect. To me, it's more effective than variable resistance training *(like Nautilus)*.

I remember when we were trying to get athletes to train with weights, the coaches wouldn't hear of it. Now all these coaches have become authorities in a year, a year and a half . . . One problem nowadays is they're putting too much emphasis on just a few things.

Like what?

Well, everything that's related to the bench press. It's nothing but a push-up lying down. It's a power exercise and very necessary, but for football players and any athletes, your power cleans, your flip snatches and your clean and jerks require quickness and ability and balance and coordination and strength. Possibly those should be given more emphasis than the bench press.

Is there much difference in the type of exercises for different sports? A football player from a volleyball player?

Well, a volleyball player has to be able to jump higher than a lineman. A lineman is big and heavy, he ain't gonna jump very high.

I guess a football player needs to be strong.

Everyone needs to be basically overall strong. For any sport you should be physically strong in the legs, arms, shoulders, chest, neck and back. You should strive to be physically strong throughout your whole body. Why should there just be strength in the shoulders and arms? Why should there just be strength in the legs? It's very simple. You analyze each *sport* and you emphasize the exercises that improve that sport's requirements. Next, you analyze each *player*, and you work to eliminate the weaknesses. That's where you start. □

Vital Statistics

Leo Stern, 65
Date of Birth: February 8, 1921
Born: Gardner, Kansas
Height: 5'8½" **Weight**: 200
Job: Owner/manager, Stern's Athletic Equipment Co. and Gyms
Lives in: San Diego, California
Activities: Walking, weight training

Wally Strauss

Wally Strauss, an internist in Mill Valley, California, encourages his patients to be physically active. The walls of his office are filled with photos of his patients running, surfing, on vacation, camping, hiking. Wally also practices what he preaches. He runs almost every day and is an outstanding competitor with best times of a 38 minute 10K and a 2:59 marathon at age 55.

You might think a serious runner like this would take his vacation lying on a tropical beach, with no running for at least a few weeks a year. Not Wally. In 1982, he and two friends spent two weeks running from Luxembourg down the Moselle River, partway up the Rhine and then (after a train ride) over the Alps. They ran about 15 miles a day. Wally's luggage for the trip weighed seven pounds, carried in a small backpack. The contents were: "Two pairs of running shoes, one dyed dark brown so we could attend the opera in Vienna, a pair of dress slacks, a white shirt, a tie and a dark sweater. Then the usual running gear: socks, shirts, shorts, a windbreaker. And one pound of paper: passports, maps, currency."

When I talked to Wally he was getting ready for another such trip. This time, "We'll be spending one week around Naples, including the Amalfi coast and a run up Mt. Vesuvius. And one week around Salzbourg again running in the Alps. Want to come?"

Vital Statistics
Wally Strauss, 59
Date of Birth: January 1, 1927
Born: Hanover, Germany
Height: 5'6" **Weight**: 125
Job: Physician
Lives in: Mill Valley, California
Activities: Running, cycling, windsurfing

My running career has been of increasing intensity over the years. I've never backed off. Temporarily, perhaps. But my daily average now is probably 10 miles. A lot of that is hill running, usually up and down Mt. Tam.

Wintertime is a problem, of course. I'm usually in the office till 5:30 and then it's dark. How do you run up the mountain in the dark? Well, I carry 2 flashlights, that's how.

Really? *(Laughter)* **Hardcore runner. What got you started running?**

Well, I started running before it became a national pasttime, about 10 years ago. I suppose it was an effort to stay in good health. To fight off old age. Prior to that I'd been an avid cyclist. And to a lesser extent, a swimmer.

You advise your patients to exercise.

Oh yes. I'm an evangelist when it comes to exercise. I think it's the essence of good health. I cajole and encourage and threaten them so they exercise. I think it's a powerful anti-depressant, a powerful anti-anxiety agent.

I was reading George Sheehan in the ***Runner*****. Everyone is always asking him if exercise helps a disease or whatever it is people have. And he said, "Run for the patient but not for the disease." In other words, it's too hard to prove that exercise will prevent people getting ill.**

You're absolutely right. The hard scientific evidence is lacking. What we are going on is soft evidence and it's really pretty shaky. And yet it's accepted. I'm a firm believer that it does good in many different areas of health. I think it keeps a person strong and vigorous and probably retards arteriosclerosis and aging. Not necessarily in everyone. But if you take a population of many people, I think the exercising individuals are in better health. And yet, if you say, "What evidence do you have for that?" I have to retreat and say the evidence is not very good. It's soft. And that's strange because so many people exercise. I suppose within a reasonably short period of time somebody will publish something that will give us a better indication that runners have less heart trouble. But even that wouldn't prove that running prevents heart trouble. It may just be that people who have less heart trouble do more running.

Do you think long-term running leads to injuries?

I think if a person is in relatively normal health, not having acute heart failure or acute angina or some kind of major orthopedic problem, running per se doesn't get you into any kind of trouble. And if you ask orthopedists, who do knee operations, "Do you usually do these operations on runners or on non-runners?" They'll say, non-runners. Running does not lead to premature wearing out of the joints or of the back. This is not to say that runners do not get knee problems. But running, all other things being the same, is far and away much more helpful than it is harmful to the human body. Let me tell you a story: This lady was employed in a chocolate factory.

She would take a ladle, immerse it into liquid chocolate, and then pour it over this glob of candy with a twisting motion of her wrist. She did this day in and day out, 8 hours a day, hundreds and thousands of these motions so that by the time she was employed for 30 years her wrist joint wore out. She did millions of these candies. O.K., joints *do* wear out. I took the number of ladling motions and multiplied that into the number of steps and number of miles that people can run. (Now this is admittedly artistic license, I don't claim it to be scientific.) If you say here's a normal joint which normally doesn't wear out, but you repeatedly traumatize it in a little way over years, it will wear out after so many millions of repetitive movements. If you use that same figure on this lady and apply it to a knee, it implies that most human beings can run 250,000 miles before their knee joint wears out. Now, nobody obviously ever runs that much. I am reminded of a lady in the Bronx who ran a marathon every day. She saw her husband off to work and at 6 o'clock she'd start running. By 10 o'clock she would have done 26 miles. A 4-hour marathon every day. She ran 16,000 miles that year. No injuries. Well, if she does that for 15 years, she may get close to wearing her joints out, but not necessarily. This is how much resilience the body has. How much repair it can do. Under normal conditions it just doesn't wear out. It's not a machine.

But you have to differentiate very carefully between a minor injury and long-term wearing out. People are afraid their bodies will wear out, that they have so many miles. Well, as I just mentioned, most people never reach anywhere near that point. Can you get injured? Sure. All you have to do is twist an ankle, there's an injury, but most people get over their groin pulls, or their shin splints or whatever is bothering them.

Why do you think so many people are physically active these days?

There is some basic physiological need for the body to move. People may have reasons why on any one day they don't want to do it, but they do it anyway. To some extent it's a growing experience of overcoming excuses. How much of an excuse are you willing to accept *not* to go out to run? I can find a dozen everyday. But there is some drive that makes us want to get out and move. Either run or play tennis or racquetball or swim or bicycle. Our modern day activity where we don't even have to turn a crank to open a tin can anymore has robbed us of this movement. And somehow the body seems to require it so it seeks these things out. That's why this is not just a fad. I'm convinced that as long as we are a sedentary society we will find ourselves exercising. Maybe 100 years from now when we don't have oil anymore and things go back to coal and the horse and whatnot, maybe exercise will lose its appeal. □

Pete Thigpen

Around noon, when many executives are downing drinks and rich food, Pete Thigpen is out running 5-10 miles along the S.F. Embarcadero and then working out on the weight machines in the Levi Strauss Fitness Center. Pete, president of Levi-Strauss' The Jeans Company, started running in 1981, ran his first marathon in 1982 in 3:06, his second soon after in 2:59 and qualified for and ran in the 1983 Boston Marathon.

To interview Pete, we headed out along the Embarcadero for Fort Point on a 12-mile run. We talked as we ran and he kept a sub-7-minute pace all the way. We came up over the hill on the way back going into Fort Mason, and then as we got within sight of the brick-clad Levi buildings Pete took off sprinting. I gave up trying to keep up with him, grumbling something to myself about the good old days, when corporate executives were fat, not fit.

What's your workout routine now?

Well, I'm kind of between marathons. Actually I'm just about to start training for New York. When I'm not working out for marathons, I'll run between 30 and 40 miles a week. What I learned from doing the San Francisco Marathon was that I lost a lot of upper body strength. My own opinion is the last 4-5 miles of a marathon, almost regardless of how much mileage you run, you're really digging down and looking for not only mental but physical strength. So I've started working the upper body a lot more.

How does your running week break down?

I do one long one on the weekends, you know, 20 miles. But on the shorter distances, I'll try to make it really high quality. Do intervals—440's, up to mile-and-a-halfs at 85 to 90% strain, trying to get up on the edge a lot more than when I just go out and chunk around and run my 7-minute miles.

How was the Boston Marathon?

The problem in Boston is between mile 16 and mile 21. There's a series of hills, the last of which is Heartbreak Hill. It's about 660 yards. The only reason that I know that is because I asked Bill Rodgers how long it was. And it *is* a heartbreaker, a real bitch. The first hill seems to be interminable and it was probably not more than 5/8 mile. You see, the first five miles is all downhill and mile 21 to mile 26 is uphill quite a ways. Once you come over Heartbreak and get into that downhill, your quads go bad on you. There have been some famous runners that have made the hill and then their quads have gone. And there are a lot of vultures waiting for you to crap out. It's painful. The *good* news is that from mile 4 to mile 26 there are crowds lining the road and of course the last 2 or 3 miles they're 8 deep on the sidewalk and you feel like Prince Charles and Lady Diana riding through the streets there. They're cheering you on—absolutely fantastic.

What did hitting the wall feel like to you?

Like you're starting to cut into muscle. You've used up your fat reserves and your whole body lets you know it. You know, the San Francisco Marathon goes by my house in two places, at 17 and then again at 21 and I was watching it last week. One of my pals came by at 17 looking pretty good, running upright and had some spring and when he came by at 21, he was visibly hunched over and suffering. He just ran out of everything. The big problem with the wall is when your mind kind of says, "Well, who gives a shit"—and "This is stupid, I don't care what my time is." You lose your morale. But in the last 3 or 4 miles you have a lot of camaraderie among the runners—you kind of help the guys along that are suffering.

What about using running for problem solving?

I'm really not very good at that. Running for me is more of a sense of self-satisfaction, of self-esteem. I feel good about myself when I'm running and after I run. And of course there's nothing quite like finishing a marathon. When I run I'm pretty much in tune with my body. I'm doing a body check on myself constantly, like a cockpit check in an airplane. I don't do much thinking out there. And I prefer to run with somebody rather than run alone even though we may not say a hell of a lot. It's stimulating and in some cases a challenge. One

Vital Statistics

Pete Thigpen, 46
Date of Birth: September 18, 1939
Born: Pasadena, California
Height: 6'2" **Weight**: 185
Job: President, The Jeans Co., Levi-Strauss
Lives in: San Francisco, California
Activities: Running, weight training, cycling, swimming, river running

Pete running New York City Marathon, 1983.

of the guys working with me has to take 8 minutes off his time to make Boston. So I'll talk to him and push him and get him to kick the last ½ mile or so, and that's good for me too.

You sometimes have meetings with people on the run.

Yeah, I do. There are guys I obviously need to meet with and time being of the essence, we'll go out and run and talk for the first couple of miles about, you know, just general things, checking off a list, things we need to cover. And then, just sitting around in the locker room, shooting the shit naked—you cut through a lot of the formalities.

What about working out in relation to your job? How about priorities?

My mental acuity is so much better when I'm running or exercising. Let me put it this way, I consider staying in shape as my first priority other than the family. So I'll schedule my workouts first and then work backwards into the business, and somehow the business always seems to get done. Whereas if I went the other way, I know I would get into business lunches and competing demands on my time. I just establish standards for myself and the people that want to see me . . . "No, I don't go out to lunch. If you want to have a lunch with me, let's go out and run."

Do you think that's something that's going to happen more and more in corporate life?

I think it better happen. For example, my father-in-law was the chief construction engineer on the Stanford Linear Accelerator and he's about 70 now and in pretty good shape himself. When he came out to watch the Corporate Cups, he said, "You know I just can't conceive of something like this taking place 20 years ago." He was really moved by the experience. He said, "Here's all these people out here, running around a track and being in shape." I think it's just become part of our culture. I think that people are getting their lives . . . I don't know if they are getting their lives in order but they are certainly setting priorities differently than they did a few decades ago. It would have been inconceivable 20-30 years ago for me to have said my first priority is working out and I work backwards into the business from there. But that's the way people are behaving now. They're just putting the value on it. The corporations are first, beginning to see that that's the way people are so they better get aboard and number two, I think corporate executives are beginning to see the value of having people that are healthy. I mean, there's a strict monetary value in terms of how much you pay for your group life and health insurance. If you have a fitness center, your insurance rates ought to come down. If you have people that are strong physically, they're going to be better workers for you.

What about your family? Does the running cause tension?

Yes and I don't know quite how to cope with that, frankly. If you figure it out, let me know. My training for a marathon takes time away from the family. Now I try to do my workouts when it doesn't interfere. I'll either run at lunch or in the morning, before everybody wakes up. But *inevitably* when you're training for the marathons, if you're going for the long ones on the weekends, it takes it out of you. A couple of ways. One, you don't want to go out partying and trashing your body on Saturday nights if you're going to run 15 miles on Sunday; so you're a little bit more cautious about cutting loose and hanging out. And second, after a 2½ hour run and a shower, you may be a little slow the rest of the day. So yes, it does cut into the family and it has created tension within. But I'm learning.

How about trips? Do you run when you travel?

First thing I do when I check into a hotel is ask for a map and find out where I can run. Sometimes it's a bit difficult because you're in the inner city. My schedulers, the people that book me into places, know what my habits are so they usually try to book me somewhere where I can run, otherwise I'm in a bad mood all day. *(Laughter).* □

Nort Thornton

Nort Thornton is an internationally acclaimed swimming coach noted for his training innovations; he has lectured in the U.S., Australia and Sweden on his techniques. In Nort's Biokinetic training room are some 20 machines, most designed to duplicate swimming motions. On the swim bench, for example, you lie down, hook your hands to paddles and . . . swim. Cables connect the paddles to an adjustable electric clutch, all monitored by a computer to read out the number of reps, length of pulls and strength put into each pull.

I first met Nort through my friend, Bill Wright, tennis coach at UC Berkeley. "You ought to see what this guy does with his swimmers," said Bill. "They work out on these machines that give them a computer read-out on their performance. They call it the torture chamber."

I wanted to ask Nort some general questions about his state-of-the-art swimming techniques that would be of interest to triathletes and master's swimmers. I also noticed that Nort had recently lost 30 pounds, looked years younger than when we first met, and had visibly more energy.

Vital Statistics
Nort Thornton, 52
Date of Birth: November 7, 1933
Born: Palo Alto, California
Height: 6'0" **Weight**: 175
Job: Swim coach
Lives in: Moraga, California
Activities: Racquetball, running, circuit training

I was feeling terrible. I just felt like I was getting so old, it was embarrassing. I couldn't stay awake, I had no energy.

I was with the Pan American team getting ready to go to South America. We spent two weeks in Florida training. Between practices, the coaches would all take off for a run. I got tired of sittin' around the hotel room waiting for 'em to come back, so I would take off with them. I'd run a minute down the beach and walk 5, and I'd just be exhausted.

I was rooming with Don Gamble, an Olympic coach from Alabama. He'd had 4-way bypass surgery and was on a real strict Pritikin diet because of it. He was religious about it. I mean, you look at that scar running all the way down there and you believe in a hurry. I watched what he was doing, listened to what he had to say and started reading about diet. So I made a change. It seemed true that your performance level would go up with a good diet. Then I figured if this can help me, it sure as hell oughta help the athletes. I started trying to push it for my team.

Well, the team talks about it and I think they're aware, but at that age they're burning it up so fast. And like with anybody, you gotta tell 'em and keep after them for years before things start happening. Sometimes it takes a crisis.

I'm not that strict with Pritikin, just tending their rules. But I'm more mentally alert and have more vitality than in years. I do weights with the kids, play racquetball and run about 3 times a week. With that and the diet, I feel much better. I can get up and go with people.

Describe your swimming program.

Swimming is a power-oriented activity. The more power you put into the water the faster you're going to move. A textbook definition of power is strength times acceleration. So strength is a factor and we use pretty standard power lifting techniques . . . free weights, Nautilus, Universal. And alternately we use Biokinetic equipment for speed lifting. These machines have speed settings on them to approximate the range of motion of swimming strokes. We go through those rapidly. We're trying to find each swimmer's power peak, where they generate the most power from zero to 10. The machine just keeps operating faster and faster and you have to work faster to keep up with it. For swimming, traditional power lifting is for general overall strength, and not very specific. What we do is start out with a strong emphasis on heavy lifting and then shift as the season goes on into speed lifting. At the end of the year we're doing our "speed circuit," the Biokinetic equipment. It's all monitored with a computer so it feeds out their mean power scores after each bout and we can adjust their duration of work.

Where's the computer attached to the swimmer?

It isn't. It's attached to the machines. The machines read the number of reps, the length of the pulls, and the strength which is put into the pulls.

So the two elements you work with are strength and speed?

Yeah. The Biokinetic equipment is for speed. I'm working on both ends

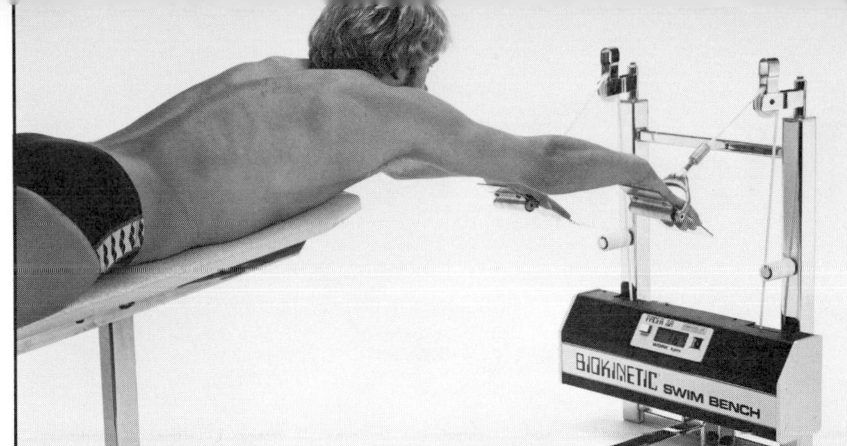

of power. Most people work only on heavy weights and I think they miss 50% of the formula.

How would you characterize the difference between bodybuilding and strength?

In bodybuilding you're trying to isolate muscle groups and bulk up the muscles. We don't want that because it's just more bulk you're pushing through the water. We hit the overall body. We do it in such a way that we don't ever get enough concentration or rest to build the muscles up. We're always tearing them down so much there's no chance for them to get too large.

You mean if you were to rest more in between the muscles would bulk up?

I think so. See, we're swimming 5 hours a day besides the hour in the weight room. I mean they're tearin' themselves apart.

I've never heard that idea before. I've heard of runners giving themselves a day of rest so muscles can rebuild.

See, the period of recovery is more important than the work itself. So we cycle our training. Like we'll do one type of training one day and the next day we'll do something entirely different. Technique work one day and the next we may swim long; the next day technique again, then we may sprint or do some aerobics. We've got a cycle which builds in some rest.

With your swimmers you're going to be real specific because it's so highly competitive. But with a swimmer who's doing triathlons, what's a general, sensible, strength program?

Well, the prime movers in swimming are the triceps. And I'm a big believer in abdominal fitness. When that's in shape, you're in shape. When that's not in shape, you've got problems. You're going to fade in a race. So do a lot of abdominal-type work and sit-ups. Keep balanced. Work muscle sets.

Is it true that in endurance swimming it's mostly upper body and the legs don't do that much?

Yes. The arms are the major movers and, of course, the legs being the biggest muscle group will tire you faster if you use them. So most people go to arm swimming and will just float the legs so they don't tire 'em. But top swimmers get their legs in shape too.

Would you tell people to do high rep stuff as they're approaching a race?

I would drop down on the heavier stuff 2 or 3 weeks before the race. Do a higher number of repetitions with lighter weights.

Can you talk about the "LSD" *(long slow distance concept used by New Zealand running coach Arthur Lydiard)* **as it applies to swimmers?**

I started reading about Lydiard and converted that into swimming a long time ago. I think you need that aerobic base . . . I kept hearing all about the specificity of training and would think, "Jeez, maybe I'm doing this all wrong." Because you get talking about guys who swim a lot to swim fast and they say, "No, you gotta swim fast to swim fast." Well, it threw me off the track for several years. And now I realize that when they talk specificity training they mean training the specificity of energy systems rather than race and actual performance speed. In other words, instead of racing fast in practice, if you want to race fast in the meet what you gotta do is train the energy system that's going to allow you to train fast (*meaning you need an aerobic base, the cardiovascular strength of endurance training as a foundation for speedwork.*) I've shifted my specificity thinking over toward the energy systems rather than speed in the water. Now they're starting to come out—I just read another Olympic Sports Medicine Committee report where they say now that you can train fast twitch muscle fibers to be endurance-oriented by long, slow distance. Then when you rest it reverts back to fast twitch, with the endurance as well. So this is something pretty new that they haven't previously believed. If that's the case, that explains why long, slow distance works. □

Mary Tiscornia

When Mary Tiscornia was a girl she loved to play baseball. "I thought the way to make boys like me was to play baseball real well. It worked for a while, but then I got to an age where it didn't really matter to the boys how well you played baseball." Mary also swam, rode a bike, ran, had a lot of energy, "... a real tomboy."

Through her teens and early 20s, Mary cut back on her athletic activity. "I was pretty shy and reclusive, plus girls in my neighborhood just didn't do those kinds of things." But in her mid-20s Mary started to run 10 miles a week, 3 months a year for several years and then decided to get serious. She increased her mileage and ran the Long Beach Marathon in 1980, at age 35, in 3:20. This qualified her to run the Boston Marathon, which she did that year. A year later she again ran Boston.

These days Mary still runs, goes helicopter skiing and horseback riding, fox hunting in Ireland and she and friend Dawn Damas have won the women's division of the Levi's Ride and Tie *6 years in a row.*

Mary lives in an old two-story farm house on a ranch in Bolinas, California with her 12-year old daughter Jennifer.

Vital Statistics
Mary Tiscornia, 41
Date of Birth: January 17, 1945
Born: Pasadena, California
Height: 5'7" **Weight:** 145
Lives in: Bolinas, California
Activities: Running, horseback riding

I always liked horses and when I could afford it I went out and bought one. And started doing some endurance riding. I was about 26.

I pretty much taught myself to ride. Then discovered that I knew how to stay on but that was all. So I took some dressage and jumping, and got involved with 3-day eventing.

What is that?

That's dressage, steeplechase, cross-country and stadium jumping inside. It takes place in 3 days on the same horse. It's one of the Olympic equestrian events. And it's a lot of fun and fairly difficult at the higher levels. I got involved in running through riding because of the first *Ride and Tie.*

Describe the *Ride and Tie.*

It's 2 people and one horse. And you leapfrog over a cross-country course that's 40-45 miles long. One person starts on the horse and the other on foot. The person on the horse rides a distance, gets off and ties the horse up and starts to run. The runner trots along looking for the horse. When they see it, they untie it, get on, and gallop to catch the running partner who's now ahead. When they catch their partner they can either pass, go farther and get off and tie, or they can do what is called a 'hand-off' where that person just jumps off and the other person jumps on.

It's really a matter of coordinating all 3 of your abilities and keeping all of your legs sound. It's not like it's a flat race course. It's up and down. Riding isn't as passive as it might appear; it takes a different set of muscles. So you basically leapfrog that way over the course and a vet checks to make sure the horse has adequate pulse/respiration recovery.

How many teams are there?

Oh, 250 maybe. And they all start like a stampede. You get a bunch of fit horses that are excited and line them up and shoot a gun. I'll tell you, you hear a lot of "Whoa, you sonofabitch" right after the gun.

What's helicopter skiing like?

It's wonderful—just being in that huge country. And you know helicopters come close to having a soul up there. They're fabulous machines. I'm not much of a machine person but I just love those darn things. They go fluttering about and that country is so beautiful.

So they'll drop you off and how long will you ski till you get picked up?

They take you out every morning at 8 and return you about 4. You generally eat lunch out in the snow.

They'll pick you up and keep taking you back up?

They take you to different runs because people like to ski fresh snow. They haul groups of 11 people, a guide and a pilot. They fly you to a spot and you ski. Maybe the snow gets bad and there's avalanche danger so they put you in different places. The last place I went—the Monashees in British Columbia—is wonderful. Gosh, I've never skied country like that in my life. It's just spectacular. I really loved it. It's so deep.... □

Riding isn't as passive as it might appear; it takes a different set of muscles.

Paul Hughes

Vince Tringali

"I've got every device known to man to get skinny," says Vince Tringali. In addition to a home full of exercise equipment, Vince practices a simple exercise that he can do sitting at his desk, driving, talking on the phone, in an airplane, anywhere: "I was laying in the steamroom one day and there's a one minute buzzer. So I said, I'm gonna hold my stomach in. Held it in a minute. Let it out, held it in. It strengthens your abdominal muscles, and that helps prevent back injuries." As we were talking, Vince tightened his stomach muscles. "Or you're driving. Use the speedometer. One mile at sixty miles an hour is a minute. Just remember to breathe."

Vince is in the advertising specialty business in San Francisco, supplying calendars, monogrammed pens, plaques, lighters, shirts, hats, hundreds of items that companies buy as gifts for employees or clients. Some of his most popular items are the calendars where he dresses up Mafioso-style and poses alongside a vintage auto.

I was born at home right here in San Francisco, and raised by the entire neighborhood. In those days, a Sicilian family had a baby, the mother went to work and everybody else took care of him. And I'm 100% Sicilian.

I played guard and tackle on the football team at USF in 1950 and '51. We had great teams, some say the finest college teams ever. Ollie Matson, Gino Marchetti, Vic Stanfill, Lloyd Barney, Joe Skidero, Ed Brown. In two years, 11 went into the pros. Unheard of.

I went back to school to complete my degree when I was thirty, and then I was head football coach at Saint Ignatius High from '59 to '69. That was really my introduction to sales. Once you're a coach, you're a salesman whether you like it or not.

You know, it's funny. When I coached that's when I would get out of shape. I just didn't have time. You get so carried away with the thing. If you take it seriously, it's a 24-hour-a-day job.

In my entire life though, I've never completely stopped working out. My intent has always been the same—to lose weight. I used to play racquetball and just do exercises, almost no weight training. Then one day I took a look at myself and said, "You know, I'm fairly slim, but I'm losing tone." I was getting the arms of (I hate to say it), an older person. I said, "Wait a second!"

Now I ride a stationary bike every morning at 5:30 for 25 minutes, then I do leg raises with 5-pound weights and I use a Total Gym. I also have a rowing machine, a slant-board, a trampoline, free weights and gravity boots. For me, the Total Gym is the most effective. It costs about $500 and packs up into a relatively small package. You can take it with you.

I've never had any trouble being motivated. None. Oh, I've stopped because of injuries. But I've always been extremely active. Even as a kid. When I stop, my body screams. It starts talkin' to me and tellin' me, "You better do something." □

Vital Statistics
Vince Tringali, 57
Date of Birth: August 1, 1928
Born: San Francisco, California
Height: 6'0" **Weight**: 212
Job: Promotional advertising distributor
Lives in: San Francisco, California
Activities: Weight training, walking, racquetball

I'm 100% Sicilian.

Charles Farruggia

Fred Van Dyke

Surfing in the '50s was a lot different than nowadays. There weren't rubber suits, so you froze. Boards were made of balsa, not foam, so you could hardly turn. There were no leashes so when you fell off you swam. Yet there was a simplicity and a purity. Surfing was uncrowded. *The cold California water in the winter kept all but the most maniacal out of the ocean. Correspondingly, there was great camaraderie; you knew all the other surfers in your area.*

In those days, if you surfed in San Francisco or Santa Cruz, you knew the Van Dykes. Doc, the father, was a dentist. Bill, the mother, was a wiry, energetic woman who never seemed to rest. And the Van Dyke kids: Fred, Gene, Gretchen and Peter, all blond, tanned, healthy and athletic, looked like an ad out of a family health magazine. All four kids surfed and spent all their spare time at the beach.

Fred moved to Hawaii in 1955, and along with Peter Cole *(see p. 34)**, Ricky Grigg, Jim Fisher, Buzzy Trent, George Downing, Wally Forsyth and others, made surfing history. They rode the biggest waves ever attempted and the first of the surfing photographers were there to record their*

Vital Statistics

Fred Van Dyke, 56
Date of Birth: April 2, 1929
Born: San Francisco, California
Height: 5'9½" **Weight:** 159
Job: Teacher
Lives in: Sunset Beach, Oahu, Hawaii
Activities: Swimming, running, cycling, surfing, hiking

Tom Sutherland

Peter Read Miller

Fred teaching creative writing class at Punahou High School, Honolulu

Tom Sutherland

Tom Sutherland

Bud Browne

Left, Fred heading for "horrendous" wipeout in 1960 at Waimea Bay, Oahu; right, with broken board same day.

feats. The photos were grainy and blurred, but the message was clear: big waves could be ridden.

Fred is a romantic, and a purist. He's pretty much given up board surfing these days as he doesn't like the crowds. Instead, Fred cycles, backpacks, bodysurfs in front of his house and swims. He's a semi-vegetarian, eats very carefully, and takes lots of vitamins and supplements.

At age 57, Fred has been teaching English and creative writing at Punahou High School in Honolulu for 30 years and is going to retire to devote more time to his writing. (He's just about to have a book of short stories published.) And what's he going to do with the rest of his time? "I'll go fishing in Montana in the summers" (where he's built himself a house) "and then I'll come back here and just become totally physical." You look at Fred, standing by the pool at Punahou, with pretty much the same broad shoulders, muscled arms, swimmer's chest he's always had—and wonder just how much more physical it's possible to become.

Why aren't you board surfing these days?

I don't like the people out surfing. Their attitude is slash, destroy, overcome the wave. My attitude is become part of the wave, feel the wave, enjoy being in that part of nature, to get lost. I'm smooth and mellow when I surf and they aren't that way and I just don't like it. It's like going from a freeway of cars to a freeway of surfboards.

It's kind of like the difference between Fred Astaire and break dancing. The kids are immensely skillful but they seem to be missing the point.

Yeah, that's it. They walk across the beach and they don't see the beach, they don't see the birds, they don't see the water, they only see a wave.

What was surfing like in the '50s in Hawaii?

Well, number one—we were pioneers. Number two—we were recluses. We were not social people. That's what put us out in the surf. Nowadays the idea is to sell clothes. It's commercial. There's movies. There's magazines. It's very social. Whereas in the '50s we were outcasts.

What's the scariest thing that ever happened to you in the big surf?

One day I went out at Avalanche with Buzzy and Al Wiemers and Pat Curren. All of a sudden this set started to march across the horizon. It was huge. Without a doubt the biggest waves I've ever been out in—30+. And I made it over the first one—it was so big that I got halfway up it and slid down backwards. And pearl dived, skeg first. I fell off the side of the board and the wave dropped right on my head. It drove me straight down. Everything turned black. I lost my equilibrium and started swimming frantically for what I thought was the surface and I was bouncing off the bottom. And I said, "Oh, shit, I'm finished. This is it. I'm in a cave. I can't get out." I was down so long before my equilibrium returned that I threw up under water—a horrendous experience, believe me. Finally I saw light above me. I made it to the surface and a second wave hit just then. And the same thing happened again. One breath in between. Then the third wave was a little easier. Then I had about a ¾-mile swim to the beach. I was sick for 3 days. Really sick. And I never went out at Avalanche again.

When did surfing start changing—with the foam?

Yeah, foam changed it. And when the mini board came, all the old ways left. And dope made a big difference—marijuana, amphetamines, mescaline.

What do you think dope does to kids?

I used to smoke it years ago. I didn't know that it wrecked your lungs. Smoking one joint, according to a UCLA researcher, is equal to smoking 20 cigarettes in regard to tar. And tar is a carcinogen.

Do you talk to kids here about it?

Yeah, I do. But most of them smoke it. It's a part of surfing, definitely.

What do you do nowadays to keep in shape?

I do interval swimming mostly. Maybe 10-20 100 yard intervals several times a week. And I run 5 miles, 3 times a week. Oh . . . and I do 100 push-ups.

All of a sudden this set started to march across the horizon. It was huge.

100 push-ups in a row?

No, I'll do 50 and whatever else it takes to get to 100. Then in a day, every time I go by a pull-up bar, I do pull-ups. So some days I might do 60-80. But not all at one time.

So you're kind of steady about what you do from week to week.

Yeah, it's pretty steady until the summertime. Then I go fly fishing in Montana and don't do much except walk up rivers.

Do you ride a bike or anything?

No, it's too dangerous. I used to but we don't have bike lanes here. And the highway doesn't have a shoulder on it. I primarily swim and run.

What do you think about the relationship of being in shape to your mental clarity and emotional health?

I think that the emotional is number one. Being in shape is secondary to emotional health and the way you eat. If you eat well and your emotions are together you won't have to do much exercise at all.

What do you do about emotions?

I meditate. I took a course called Silva Mind Control and you learn how to get to the Alpha level. I meditate every day. Sometimes as little as 5 minutes, sometimes an hour or two, anywhere I can just be quiet and close my eyes. It's very important to me.

That's the emotional part. What about the dietary part? Do you eat red meat?

No. The only time is when I go visit my mother and she'll say, "OK, I know you two are vegetarians so I'll have a stew tonight." She'll have a vegetable stew with meat in it so you can't avoid it. I eat fish and not much chicken. Normally we eat a lot of fruits and vegetables and an awful lot of tofu.

Bud Browne

Fred at left, Waimea Bay, 1964.

And you take vitamins every day?

Yes. I take an overdose of B-vitamins continually. And brewer's yeast. And I take B-12.

No coffee?

No coffee. I have one bad habit—I drink beer. Foreign beer—not that American junk.

What will you do with all your time when you retire?

I'm going to write, I'm going to surf, run, swim, windsurf—I'm going to have all day long to do these things and I'm going to just push my body as far as it will go. □

Len Wallach

When Len Wallach took over as race director for S.F.'s Bay to Breakers *race in 1979, it was about to be cancelled. Using the leadership he'd learned in working his way from a private to a major in the U.S. Army, Len orchestrated the transformation of the* Bay to Breakers *into what is now the world's largest footrace: some 75,000 runners.*

Leadership is a word that comes up often in Len's conversation. He's fascinated by the accomplishments and subtleties, the craft of good leadership. It's a quality he obviously knows something about: besides handling the Bay to Breakers, *Wallach was the Olympic Marathon Director in 1984, with a total of 4000 people working for him.*

Len talks fast and is excited about all his current projects. He's written a book, The Human Race, *and is working on another:* Quarterbacking the Winning Team: Leadership in an Organization. *He writes a weekly newspaper column and carries his office around with him in the form of a small black binder with addresses, phone numbers, all his appointments, notes on all his projects: "It takes the place of all the office furniture, the rug on the floor, the painting on the wall and it works!"*

I met Len at the snack bar at the U.S. Army Presidio base in S.F. for lunch. We never did *talk about what Len does to keep in shape. (He runs, of course–but for enjoyment, not competition.) Instead, he talked about The Winning Team, his latest venture, what he sees as the real values and rewards of life and the relationship of sports to success in the business world.*

Vital Statistics
Len Wallach, 59
Date of Birth: December 6, 1927
Born: Scofield Barracks, Oahu, Hawaii
Height: 5'10" **Weight**: 161
Job: Special events
Lives in: San Mateo, California
Activities: Running

The Winning Team stages special events and instructs companies in leadership skills. We can go into any kind of company, give us two hours, and we'll give you skills that will improve productivity, smooth out your operation and give you better direction.

Sports is a device that illustrates our concepts. Tenacity is a characteristic of sports. How do you make somebody tenacious in business? First of all, you get 'em healthy. Productivity is directly related to health. You can skip all the bullshit about smoking doesn't hurt you. It does. It hurts you bad. Poor nutrition hurts you bad. Frustration with your wife hurts you bad. You've got to be healthy. If you're not and you think you can compete with the guys who *are* healthy, you're dead wrong. Any corporate executive having two martinis per lunch and scarfing down the food is a fool. If you're going to make a major business decision during that lunch or assess somebody, eat before you go so you're not playing the other guy's game. You can't eat and think at the same time. A simple rule. Any soldier knows that. That's why they don't feed troops before they go into combat.

Number two, sexual search. Males spend 90% of their time trying to get laid. That means they're taking 90% of their time away from business. So they gotta be told, "You don't do that. If you're not getting enough at home, don't bring it to the marketplace." And if you're a coquettish woman playing that provocative game, we recommend you knock it off.

The Winning Team is a new approach for corporations. We're not going to have people go off and contemplate their navels in some exotic retreat. This is a 2-hour block of instructions with brown bag lunches. We'll take say 15 executives and get them together and say, "These are the kinds of qualities a leader has. Here are the pitfalls. Sexual search is a pitfall." And while we're describing this, some people in that room are going to be

Gene Sohn

very uncomfortable because we're describing them. We don't have to say a thing. We have 100 different subjects we're going to hit in those two hours. And because people tend to have a hard time remembering inspirational things, we'll back it up with a book they can refer to.

The greatest lesson a businessman can learn: If you do the rest of it right, the money will come. You do the basics wrong, the money will never come. If you don't tell the truth, it'll bite you on the ass. The thing about the world of commerce that fascinates me is that the very thing you want the most is the thing that's going to destroy you. If money is your ambition, then money is going to destroy you.

If I had my way, I'd get rid of all the damn medals for races. Look, achievement is appropriate. Recognition is appropriate. But if you're so goddamn immature that you have to have the stroke every time you have the achievement, you're pretty immature. If you said to me, "Name ten things that are important to you," I would reel off my 6 children and my wife as the first seven things, OK? I have the ultimate reward, the poor man's reward, children. They're good kids who have character and insight into the world they live in, and appreciation for compassion and tenderness and charity—all those virtues. That's not mom and apple pie, that's real.

Ever been up to Laguna Honda Hospital, the rest home in San Francisco? Go up there and look at some of those poor, homeless people sometime. They have no family, nothing. If you can get to the point where you can do something like visit those people, it doesn't make any difference how far you can run or how much power or money you've got. The fact that you're charitable, I mean charitable with your time when it's hard to do, that's an achievement. They say virtue is its own reward.

People who seek only to acquire power or possessions are fooling themselves. My wife and I took a kind of half-assed vow of poverty, chastity and obedience. That is, we don't want to own anything that we don't absolutely need. We spend our money on the things we need to spend money on and if we've got any left we put it to useful purpose. Charities. Benefitting people that need it.

Even my military decorations have been given away because at some point in your life you say that stuff's not really important. What's important is a whole bunch of other things. In my case, it's my family, my religion, my self-development and understanding really, how inadequate I am. See those pictures of the catacombs of Rome and those skeletons stuffed in those caverns? That's what you are. That's where you're going to wind up. Now, you pass through this earth, maybe with a purpose, maybe without a purpose. I really don't know. But you can spend 20 years saving your money and being nice and secure in your goddamn little house with the green lawn, and when you wake up you're 65 years old and doddering around in Honolulu with spindly little white legs and a pair of Bermuda shorts lookin' like an asshole. If you want to be a prisoner for your whole life, that's fine, but don't waste your time looking for security. The only real security is in yourself.

The thing that's great about the *Bay to Breakers* is that it's frivolous. It's something that you want to go to, a thing that has a lot of humanness in it. You behave on race day the way you should behave the rest of the year. It's a reflection of the spirit of San Francisco, a statement to the hotshots not to take yourselves so seriously because we're gonna forget you tomorrow. □

Ivor Welch

Robin Welch

Here's a man born in 1895 who took up running in 1977. He enjoys the people he's met running, the fresh air, the scenery, and the consequent strong heart, lungs and body. He says there's a bit of ego involved, but he only competes with himself to do the best he can. At age 91 he's still running in races and hopes to run his sixth marathon this year. And being a San Francisco resident, he always runs the Bay to Breakers.

I came from a small town in Missouri. I was just an ordinary kid. In 1913 I went to Chicago and studied art at the Art Institute. When World War I came along I enlisted in the Army, in 1917. I went to France then came back to Chicago after the war. Found out I had tuberculosis and I came West. In those days the thought was to go West when you had the Great White Plague. I had sense enough to do what the doctors at the hospital told me to do. So I eventually beat it. Whereas many other young fellas no worse than I was died.

What was it they had you do?

No drinking, smoking, or carousing. Rest. All of which I did very religiously. I lived in the dry climates of New Mexico and Arizona until 1934, when I came to California.

Vital Statistics
Ivor Welch, 91
Date of Birth: January 19, 1895
Born: Moscow Hills, Missouri
Height: 5'6" **Weight**: 145
Job: Retired
Lives in: Pacifica, California
Activities: Running, hiking, hunting, fishing

Were you doing any exercising during those years?

I have always been an active person, never sedentary, even when I was a tubercular patient. As soon as the doctors would permit I got out to walk. At first just short, but I gradually increased to two hours a day. Later they allowed me to do a little horseback riding. I've always liked to walk. I've been a hiker, backpacker, hunter, fisherman, roamed the hills. That sort of thing. In the desert country there was much to do and see. And I did as much as I could of it.

When did you start running?

It was in 1977, I was 82 years old. In about 1975, my wife contracted cancer. During the last couple of years I had to devote myself almost full-time to taking care of her. When she died, in September, 1977, I was devastated. Pretty much at loose ends. I'd go out for my usual walks and I saw an awful lot of people running. I wondered if an old man could run. So as I walked, I would run a few steps. I went and had a thorough medical examination, got a clearance, then I started to walk a bit and run a bit. Gradually increased it until a year and a half after I started it I did my first marathon.

How long did it take you?

Six and a half hours. I arranged with the director ahead of time to start four hours early. Two men passed me within the last half mile of the finish line, and I came in third, which looked like quite an accomplishment for an old man. I got a lot of applause. But then they announced that I had started early. Still, I was naturally pleased with myself, that I had finished. I've run four more since and each one I've cut off a little time. I did the Avenue of the Giants the next year in 5:58. Then I did the Sri Chimnoy in 5:55. My best time was 5:40 when I did the Avenue again.

How old were you?

87.

You also ran the Pike's Peak run?

I did the ascent, which is 14 miles. It's the toughest of any because of the altitude. I've done 20-milers, 10-milers, 25 kilometers and 10K's. I've done the *Bay to Breakers* six times now. I'm always the oldest, if not the fastest.

What's your typical week of running?

I'm kind of a free runner. Some weeks I'll do 20 miles, some 10, some 30. No regular schedule. Actually I'm a walker who runs a little. Not a runner who walks a little. I enjoy the physical exertion and being out in the open and seeing and thinking. I realize that it's also beneficial from a heart and lung point of view. Then there's always the ego involved. But I don't compete with other people because I have sense enough to know that at 90 I can't compete with a 60-year-old man. But I can at least compete with myself and do the best I can. I am hoping to do another marathon this year after my 90th birthday.

Do you like the people you've met running?

I think they're above the average. Because they are people who not only have jobs and work but they are people who realize they've got to do something else in order to live.

At 90 I can't compete with a 60-year-old man. But I can at least compete with myself and do the best I can.

Robin Welch

Robin Welch

So many people will do various athletics in school, then get married and get a job and so forth, and then spend 20 or 30 years during their middle life doing nothing . . . until they and their friends begin having heart attacks and high blood pressure. So then they start doing things. A lot of the runners you meet today are 40 and older. They're a nice bunch of people.

What do you do about diet? Have you had any habits all your life that have helped you out?

Well, I don't say all my life because one learns as he gets older. But for many years I've been a semi-vegetarian. I eat meat maybe once a week but I don't crave it. I catch myself eating only my fruits and vegetables and then having to eat my meat consciously. I mostly eat fruit, vegetables, cereals, milk, cheese, that sort of thing.

Just because you like them?

And because I think they're better for me. My blood pressure has always been quite good. I had a check for cholesterol not long ago. After the test I called the man at the hospital and he said, "Yeah, it's normal." I said, "What's normal? I want the figures." So he said, "OK, 240." Doctors will tell you that anywhere from 100 to 300 is normal. But Pritikin and others say your cholesterol should be your age plus 100 but not over 150-160. So I have recently been eating almost no meat and none of the things which have cholesterol. And I'm sure it will drop below 240.

Do you take supplements?

Yeah, a few vitamins. And I have for quite some time now been taking bee pollen, which they make great claims for. So far I can't see any important effect but I'm still checking it. There's a man named Noel Johnson down in San Diego who promotes bee pollen. He has written a book *At 70, A Dud; At 80, A Stud. (Laughter)* He makes great claims for it. Well, maybe at 70 it works. At 90, so far it hasn't. *(Laughter)* But who knows. □

Sherman Welpton

Lloyd Kahn, Jr.

Sherman Welpton was a minor celebrity in his college days (Stanford) for being able to take what appeared to be bone-crunching falls and survive unharmed. He and a friend would often stage mock fights at the top of the stairs in the Fiji House, Sherm would get hit with what looked (and sounded) like a hard right to the jaw, and he would roll, bang and bounce down the stairs with groans of pain and collapse in a heap at the bottom. When observers were about ready to call an ambulance, he'd bound up laughing.

To do these stunts Sherm was obviously a good athlete and in excellent physical condition. He practiced judo, was a light-heavyweight boxer, a rope climber and had run the 440 in 50.3 in high school in Los Angeles.

I lost track of him for some time after college, until about ten years later when I saw him at a party. He'd gained so much weight I hardly knew him. Then for another 10 years I didn't run into him. One day my brother sent me a newspaper article: Sherm had just run his 100th marathon! I called him with the idea that his experiences and transformation might make a good book. When we got together we started talking about friends who still tried to keep in shape, and about the excitement we all found in our lives by staying physically active. This eventually led to Over The Hill.

Sherm has now run 140 marathons. He has taken 40-50 people through their first marathons, including his son Blake who, at age 11, finished in 5:03. Sherm has a best time of 3:10 in 1979, has done 18 50-milers, four 100-milers (28 hours of continuous running in the Sierras), has brought his weight down from 225 to 175 and is very much alive, kicking and... running, swimming, cycling and tap dancing.

Vital Statistics

Sherman Welpton, 51
Date of Birth: June 6, 1934
Born: Omaha, Nebraska
Height: 6'0" **Weight**: 175
Job: Municipal bond broker
Lives in: Oakland, California
Activities: Running, tap dancing

How did you get into running?

Actually, it was a return to what worked best because I had run in high school. I wasn't a basketball or baseball player. I wasn't gonna go out and join an evening league of pick-up softball. But I had always walked and run.

Did any incident start you off?

It was a combination of events. At the time I was going through a divorce and quitting my job as stockbroker. Quitting hard liquor and heavy food. All those things happened within about a 90-day period. I just looked at my life and was very dissatisfied.

Tired of being a stockbroker?

Yeah, I looked at where I was and said, I'm coming home every night under a lot of pressure to a wife who is a pleasant person but we have nothing in common anymore, we're strangers in the same house, looking at each other. To two kids who had become an obligation, a duty because of all the other pressures I had. I weighed 225 lbs. I huffed and puffed when I got up the hill from the bus station and I just said, hey, I don't know what's going to work in the future but this doesn't work. I need to get out of the stock brokerage business and do something I not only make money at but enjoy. Prior to that I used to confuse accomplishment with success. It was a big decision I had to make in my life. I didn't want to just do something for money each day. I wanted to do something I liked and that was also useful to others. At the same time I said, I can't weigh this much and enjoy myself. So I fell back on my walking. My doctor said, "You're so heavy, Sherman. You need to walk before you run." You see, running was just beginning to be popular.

I started walking in October, 1977. My first race was on Valentine's Day in February, 1978, a 10K, twice around Lake Merritt. I did my first marathon in July of 1978—the San Francisco marathon.

Within 8 months you were running a marathon, weighing over 200 lbs.?

I was still overweight and out of shape. I had to walk and run and run and walk. I finished it in 5 hours and 3 minutes. But I was so delighted to be on a new course of action.

So you first walked?

Yeah. I walked for 3 months. Then I started to jog and by February ran that first 10K race, very slow. Something like 11-minute miles. I was out there forever. When I finished I was so happy. I called my parents, I called my brother and sister. I told them I had actually run 6 miles. After that I was really addicted. I just felt so good. I would come home and change into my running clothes and jog out the front door and run 5-6 miles a night. It felt so good to break those habits, that constantly coming home and having a scotch and soda with dinner and some heavy meal. Instead I'd fix up a little tuna salad.

What do you do now? You run after work usually?

Usually after work at night. During the summer I start at 10 and run to 11 or 11:30 at night.

With reflectors on?

Yes, around Piedmont and Oakland.

Do you eat dinner after that?

Yes, usually something very light. You know when it's so hot during the day and you come home and work out, it's very uncomfortable. I've never been a morning runner. In the marathons and the competitive runs you get up and run on a Saturday or Sunday morning but I find if I run weekdays early in the morning I get very anxious about getting to work late as my business starts at 7 A.M. So it destroys the enjoyment of the run. Also, many times it saps that critical energy I need early in the morning. I like to run best at the end of the day when I'm absolutely exhausted.

How much are you running now? Does it vary?

Not much now, maybe 40-50 miles a week. It's been much higher, like 80-90 miles a week when I was getting ready for the Western States run.

What do you anticipate doing in the future?

I'm bicycling and swimming now. I'm really pointing toward the Ironman Triathlon in October, 1986.

You'll be 52 then?

Yes, exactly. One of the things I found when I kept running at a given level, it started to get boring. I wanted to change that so I'll always look forward to the run and not have it become a workout I've got to get through with. I want to make sure that life is as much as it can be for me—always an adventure. Keep changing the routine. What I did was to use running to take control of my life and now I use it to keep challenging myself.

That's good. It all ties together.

Yeah. Likewise, you know the investment business allows you a wide latitude. You can do commodities, options, stocks, bonds, mutual funds, municipal bonds, anything you want within the framework of dealing with a raw product called money. The important ingredient to me is that what I do is useful to other people. I'm in the municipal bond business now and extremely proud of the fact that my clients have been to my

Camille Welpton

Ruth Boyer

1977, Sherman at 220 pounds, and... in 1980 finishing 100 mile race at 175 pounds.

Steve Jaber

talks or classes or are referrals. They're not my customers because I've pressured them with a lot of phone calls.

There have been a tremendous number of lessons that have come out of running that I've applied to the rest of my life. One of the most important is integrity, that promises made to myself about running and diet are kept, they're "bankable." For me it was the cornerstone of self-respect. I also think that integrity, like honesty, is a battle that's fought every day in the trenches and not paved over at the end of life with donations and monuments.

Secondly, running was exciting and I had the fear of failing and not finishing a race and all those kinds of things. But the truth is it was non-threatening. It was not life and death. In business on the other hand I felt I had to succeed. I could accomplish a lot in running I couldn't in business. Then lo and behold, I applied these lessons and all of a sudden business was no longer threatening... it was fun. And now I'm getting a lot accomplished in business because of that.

Any other lessons from all this?

Well, what I began to see very clearly about the kind of life that *doesn't* work that became very clear in running that *does* work is the whole thing of what you think about yourself. It isn't a case of how much money or how many Porsches, or where you live... you know, all of that kind of stuff. It's really a case of self-evaluation. My brother, who is a psychiatrist—he's one of the few shrinks I know that doesn't need to be strapped down himself *(Laughter)*—he and I got talking here about two years ago when I'd gone to the Boston Marathon the third time and spent some time really getting reacquainted and really lashing our brotherhood together again. He said to me, "The bottom line, Sherman, in psychiatry, that I've come to after all these many years, is that life is really nothing more than what we think of ourselves. When life doesn't seem to go right for us, I'm convinced that we're punishing ourselves." Taking command of our own lives, that's

Nancy Saunders and Susan Chamberlain

John Chamberlain, Sherman, James Saunders, 1979 – Mayor's Cup Marathon, San Francisco.

Brock Settlemier

Joan Szarfinski, Sherman tap danced through 1979 Bay to Breakers Race in San Francisco.

what the bottom line is: we're responsible for what we're doing to ourselves every day.

You know, whether people are into triathlons or running or aerobic dancing or whatever it is . . . What I see happening more and more in this country is that people are getting away from some habits that developed mostly out of ignorance. I don't really think people would eat a lot of heavy food and drink a lot of hard liquor if they knew they could have just as good a time in athletics.

If you could just get people to—without injuring themselves—get the feeling of what it's like to be a live animal and to be in shape, like any wild animal is. Once they're there for the second time in their lives, there's a pretty good chance they're not going to let it slip again.

Right. Because I see people get in their 40s, 50s and 60s and get very self-destructive out of low self-esteem. Once you change that and go back into the second good feeling like being a kid again, and get that muscle tone, you feel how much more you can do. Without even thinking about it you've got another hour to two hours worth of energetic work or activity or excitement or enjoyment every day without feeling logy. Now I get to go to bed without getting up in the morning and swallowing two aspirins and an alka seltzer to get the pump started.

In deciding to stay fit, you're taking control.

Right! You know, one of the things I've always wanted to do, I mean don't ask me why—everybody's got their Idiot Savant I guess. One thing I've always wanted to do is go out in front of an audience and tap dance. *(Laughter)*

Have you tried it?

Yeah. I started tap dancing about the same time that I started running. I tap danced for about one year and the running got so intense that I put the tap dancing away and then recently when I hit my 100th marathon I got the shoes off the shelf and started back in. When I first started the tap dancing, before the running and before a lot of those insights I was so uptight about—how do you move your legs, what do you do and, like playing a game of golf, by the time you remember how your grip is and everything else you never even get the goddamn swing up off the ground. I was this way with tap dancing. I was so uptight about remembering routines and making a mistake, pissed off at myself at forgetting routines and patterns.... Well, now here I am four years later, back into this thing and it's going much better because I'm just out to dance and have a good time. You see, I never went into running with any great expectations at the time, just to exercise, lose weight and all the other things came around pretty well. I'm still not a sub-three-hour marathoner, but I have a good time, do everything I want to do, and am not uptight about whether my split times are up with Bill Rodgers.

You know I used to play the ukelele in high school and at Stanford and then I kinda gave it up. I felt, well Jees it's not very hip. I should learn to play the guitar and I struggled with the guitar for years. Then just about a year ago I was walking past a second-hand shop and saw a ukelele and I bought it and I've just been having the greatest time with it. I'm not worried about being like Andre Segovia anymore. The kids love it.

All *right,* bring out that Sweet Georgia Brown. *(Laughter)*

Where do you go for lessons?

There's a studio in Oakland, Tappin' Fancy. They have a show every June and my goal is to be one of the real contributors. This is a lifetime fantasy come true. The old Welps up there in the tap dancing shoes.... Five years ago when I first started this thing, I was still about 200 pounds. I hadn't broken through yet. So, when you put the Levi cords on and the t-shirt and your tap dancing shoes and your gut hangs out over your belt like a long-haul truck driver, and you're looking in the mirror at your feet and going back and forth, *(laughter)* you don't have a great image of yourself. But when you're at 175 and you're moving around like that, all of a sudden you say, shit, "Look *out,* Fred Astaire!" □

Jack Fulton

Sherman's race T-shirt collection.

Lillian White

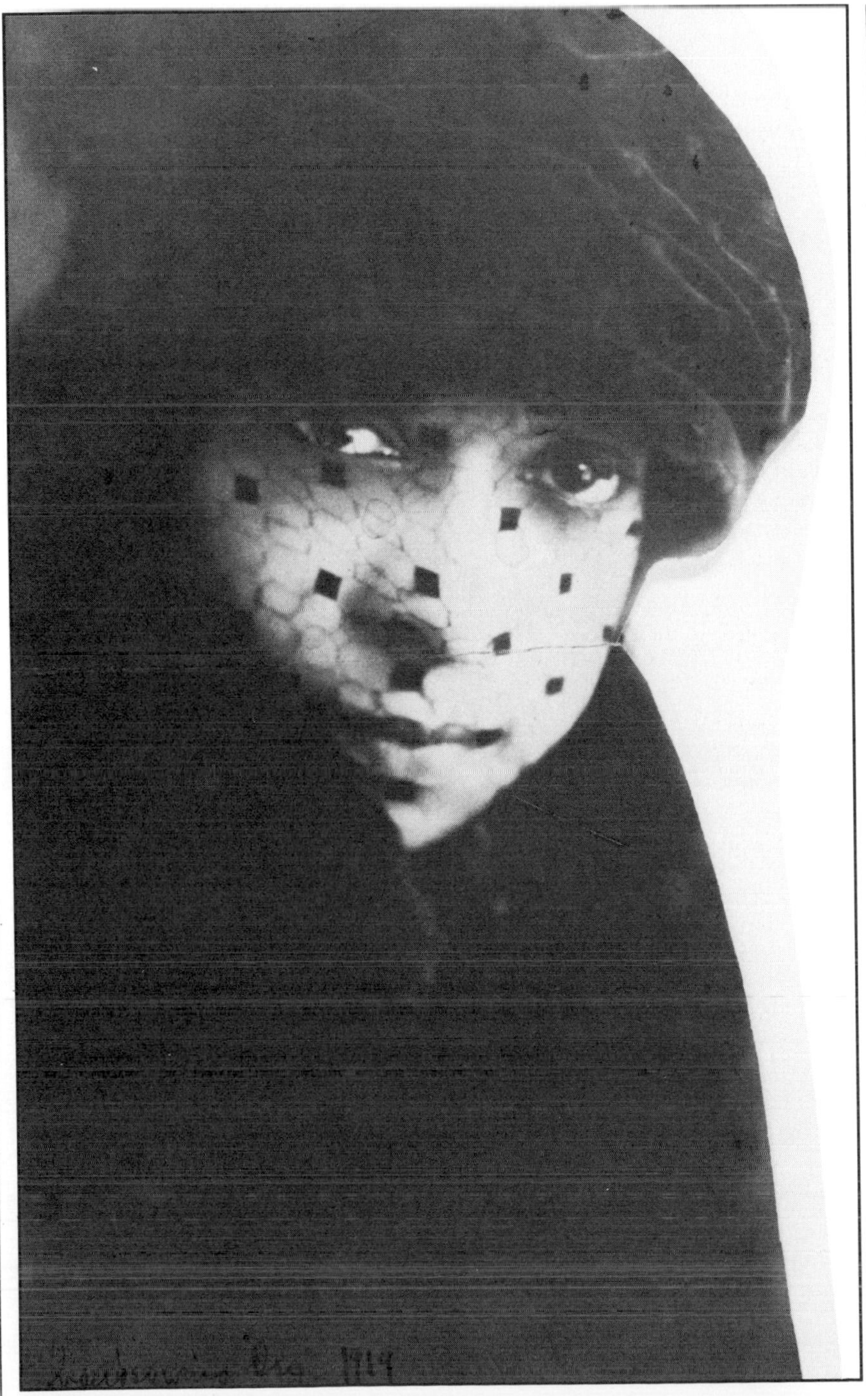

Lillian, left, and husband Uriah, above, at courtship age

Lillian White turned 100 in 1985. She is formal and dignified, elegant in a way that only beautiful old women are. You recognize her from a distance by her striking white hair and high-heeled, knee-high boots, her red leather purse, a scarf, her smile. Talking to her, you begin to feel yourself grow calm in her presence; she has a way of listening to you thoughtfully before she answers. She is precise and cheerful, at ease in her body, mannered and graceful.

She lives in San Francisco with her husband Uriah (a younger man at age 92), in a tenth-floor apartment with a magnificient view of the city and the bay. Asked how long they've been married, Uriah and Lillian look at each other and try to place the date but they can't agree, except that it has been a long time.

–Marianne Orina

I just love to wear nice clothes and jewelry. And the other thing is, I don't take life too seriously.

Marianne Orina

Uriah and Lillian in 1985

Marianne Orina

What are some of your secrets to your long and healthy life?

It was a very pleasant life. My father and mother lived to be up in years. They reared their children, then my aunt took me and gave me a musical education at the New England Conservatory of Music. I was a child prodigy on the piano. I spent a number of years with my aunt. She was an entertainer, a musician. I lived with people who were musicians. I played the pipe organ in the church. People who came to Boston, I played for them; at concerts I was the accompanist.

Did you do a lot of exercise during the course of your life?

Oh yes. I loved animals and I trained animals, dogs, horses. I rode horses, and bicycles.

You rode horses every day?

I loved it. Every day. I rode frequently. A friend introduced me to riding. She had been riding for a number of years. Then when they finally had a horse show she got second prize and I beat her. She never got over it.

What do you do right now to keep fit?

At my age, you don't do anything but just try to live. I eat. I have a good appetite. The doctor told me not to increase my appetite, not to eat any more. I eat a lot of grapefruit and vegetables. Grapefruit is a wonderful fruit.

Vital Statistics

Lillian White, 100
Date of Birth: October 29, 1885
Born: New Bedford, Massachusetts
Job: Retired social worker
Lives in: San Francisco, California
Activities: Walking

I drink coffee when I go out, just to have a friendly chat, you know.

Do you consciously avoid things like sweets and coffee?

I don't drink coffee at home. I drink coffee when I go out, just to have a friendly chat you know. But here at home I drink tea.

Did you ever smoke cigarettes?

I tried. I did have one pack one time and then I said I'm not going to spend any more money on cigarettes.

What about alcohol?

I'll take a drink occasionally. But I'd never overdo it.

Where are your parents from?

My mother was a Native American Indian, Naragansett. My father was born in New Bedford, Massachusetts. He's an American.

What kind of food did you eat growing up?

My mother could cook. She could cook, anything we could eat and we loved her food.

What kind of food?

Plain but good.

You ever do any gardening?

In Boston we had a house with an adjoining garden and my people used to plant corn, vegetables. We'd eat salad right out of the garden. I think spinach is one of the best foods you can eat.

Did you not eat too much meat?

Not too much. Just fish.

Tell me some of your beauty secrets.

Oh. *(Laughter)* I just love to wear nice clothes and jewelry. And the other thing is, I don't take life too seriously.

What kind of work did you do?

I worked for United Charities, Planned Parenthood, as a counselor. When I retired they gave me a pension which has run out since. I outlived it.

Was that part of your decision not to have any children?

No. I wanted children, I just never had any.

How did you and your husband meet?

Well, let's see. That was in Chicago. We met through a friend of mine who knew him. Uriah was like a little Indian boy. I was in love with him, I guess, more than he was in love with me. But I convinced him. I followed him around and took him with me and introduced him to friends. I courted him first, then we courted each other. It was just a lovely friendship. We finally got married in Las Vegas.

What was your wedding like?

It was very matter of fact. You can get married quick in Las Vegas.

What did you do for fun?

We used to go to the horse races and play the horses. That was a good part of our friendship. Though my husband never went on the back of a horse in his life. But I know horses. Once you've been on the back of a horse, he knows you and he knows you the next time. There's some horses, you get on their back and they'll throw you off because they don't know you. You pick 'em, certain horses they like you and they'll be just as mild and tame as anything else. That's an animal knowing you.

How has the world changed over the course of your lifetime, with all the inventions we have now?

New Bedford in the old days was just a quaint country town. So we did a lot of walking. My grandfather had a horse and wagon and I loved to ride into town on that. The telephone and the car and television, things like that, you just accept them as they come. I've taken a few plane rides. I once drove from Los Angeles (my sister lived in Los Angeles) to Boston. We had to get on a boat in Detroit to get to Buffalo, New York. It took you all night to do that.

What are your plans for the future?

You know, my friend Helen tells me how she keeps up with her good health, she takes a hot bath every night. I thought I should try that. □

Bill Wilson

Billy Wilson looks pretty much the same as he did in high school, except for the grey hair. Billy was a swimmer and surfer through high school and college, but when he started teaching he quit working out for ten years. He had small kids, worked hard at his job, smoked, drank coffee, developed back problems and finally found out that he had high blood pressure and high triglycerides.

Because of that Billy started exercising again: swimming and working out on a Universal weight machine. He once again surfs, on weekends, during summer and on a once-a-year trip to Oahu's North Shore. He also swims in the annual Golden Gate Bridge swim and competes in run/swim events each summer. In 1984 he was the fastest over-50 swimmer in the Berkeley Iron Horse Triathlon.

Billy has some good ideas about endurance swimming and training for triathlons.

During the school year I swim maybe 4 or 5 times a week—about an hour straight of swimming usually amounts to about a mile and a half. I don't work out hard. I've experimented and interval training just makes me tired. By interval training I mean speedwork. Long slow distance with just a little bit of speedwork seems to be the best.

You really have to divide up hard days and easy days. One day I'll work with a paddle and a kick-board so I'm working my legs and arms, kinda overloading them. On those days I do long slow distance in between the paddles and kicking. Then the days I do speedwork I also swim the other strokes—breaststroke, backstroke and butterfly.

What's a good training program for a 1-1½ mile triathlon swim?

There are a few general things that over-40 swimmers should always remember. You should warm up thoroughly and with a stroke that keeps your arms in the water, say breaststroke. You have to get the rotator muscles warm before you can do your crawl effectively and without risk of injury. Also, it takes older swimmers longer to get their rhythm. So swim the first five minutes without worrying about times. Just get the feel of the water. Glide along until you begin to sweat and you get into your breathing cycle. You shouldn't do the hard part of your workout until about the midpoint of your time in the water.

But specifically, the most important thing is to do your long distance (1-1½ miles a day, 3 times a week), at the beginning of the season and then start working into your intervals. You can't jump into interval training. You'd be nauseated if you tried to do five 200's when you hadn't been swimming for a couple of months. Here's a good guideline: When the long, slow distance becomes too easy, when you can do a mile easily, start your intervals. Start with 200's or 500's if you're training for a 2K triathlon swim.

Begin your speedwork. Don't decide to increase your distance swimming instead. That's when you develop bad habits like reaching out too far, dropping your elbow, turning your head too far to breathe. These things make it easier but they slow you down. That's what too much long, slow distance will do.

What about working on your kick?

You don't want to kick in a triathlon swim, because you'll pay for it in the biking and running. If you kick hard, your legs are going to be jelly-like for the rest of the race and you could cramp. Most good triathlon swimmers use a two-beat rather than a six-beat kick.

Any tips on technique?

The most common mistake of anyone who started swimming in the '50s or before is that we were told to pull with our arms straight and not to let them weave. Just pull it straight back. Now, they realize that an "S" stroke is the most efficient. The best thing is to go and get a good coach and do some stroke drills. But if you're working on your own, think of pushing the water at all times toward your feet. When you're doing it right, you feel you're actually picking up speed at the end of the stroke, like you're going downhill. If you feel like you're swimming uphill, you're doing it wrong. □

Vital Statistics

Bill Wilson, 51
Date of Birth: November 21, 1934
Born: San Francisco, California
Height: 5'8" **Weight:** 140
Job: Teacher
Lives in: El Cerrito, California
Activities: Swimming, surfing, weight training

50 year old surfers Jack Roddy, left, and Billy.

Billy, left and José Angel in Hawaii in the '50s.

Lloyd Kahn, Jr.

Billy in 1984 Run-Swim-Run Race in Santa Cruz, California.

Bill Wright

Bill Wright is an adventurous athlete. Coach of the men's tennis team at the University of California at Berkeley, Director of Tennis at Vail, Colorado during summers, and the author of Aerobic Tennis, *Bill plays tennis daily, runs in races, goes to aerobic dance classes (with his team), lifts weights, is currently taking a course in Korean karate, periodically hangs upside down from his gravity inversion boots, surfs on a boogie board, and sometimes jumps in the ocean for a swim in the winter at 6:30 A.M.*

Whenever a new, antique or wacky fitness device comes up for sale, Bill will buy it. "Some people collect paintings, I collect weightlifting stuff." You have to walk sideways in his garage past the strange-looking machines and exercising apparatus and his backyard is filled with barbells, benches, hanging ropes and a home-made obstacle course. Here is a partial list of Bill's exercise equipment (believe it or not): a squat rack, a quad/hamstring machine, dipping bars, hanging rings, a homemade stretching machine, a rowing machine, an exercycle, a mountain bike, a racing bike, a Bullworker, a 5-pound jumprope, a sports stick, and gravity boots. Bill's large van is filled with tennis gear, basketballs, a medicine ball and his surfboard.

Bill grew up on a ranch in Wyoming and started playing tennis when he was 12. At age 14 he used to get up at 5 A.M. to hit balls against the wall of a nearby office building. He went to college at Southern Methodist University in Dallas, then got his law degree in Denver. He practiced law for 5 years in Los Angeles before returning to his true love, tennis. In 1974 he was ranked number 7 in the U.S. in the 35-and-older category. In 1978 he was picked the NCAA coach of the year and in 1980 his Cal Bears won the national indoor team championship.

Vital Statistics
Bill Wright, 47
Date of Birth: December 30, 1937
Born: Atlanta, Georgia
Height: 5'7" **Weight**: 145
Job: Tennis coach, author
Lives in: Moraga, California
Activities: Tennis, running, bicycling, basketball, weight training, hiking, Idaho surfing*
**Tethering a piece of plywood to a bridge in a swiftly moving stream*

I've always thought there was a tremendous correlation between playing good tennis and strength. Until recently, with the exception of Harry Hopman *(the famous Australian coach),* nobody else was using weights or emphasizing strength training.

I started lifting weights when I was in college. I still have my copy of *Better Athletes Through Weight Training.* It was by Bob Hoffman and was the first weightlifting book for athletes. I'd lift weights, climb the rope in the gym, do dips on the parallel bars. I even went to the Charles Atlas studio and bought the whole course. I wasn't gonna let a big guy kick sand in *my* face at the beach.

Were you pretty good in high school?

I was the best player in Wyoming. But that's not saying much. I think there were 4 of us. Cheyenne had six tennis courts and is no country club town. To hit balls by myself, I'd prop up these 6 by 6 pieces of plywood against a sawhorse. I'd stretch a net across two fenceposts in a creekbed, and I'd have a practice board. It was terrific. I called it Redstone Tennis and Swim Club. When someone from Denver would stop in and hit a few balls . . . well, I'd think he was the greatest player in the world. I'd copy him. And a lot of these guys weren't very good.

In college at SMU, I had to play with and against guys from Texas and California who had a lot more experience. By the time I was a senior, we won the Southwest Conference team championship, and I was part of the championship doubles team, and a finalist in singles. Strength and conditioning were a great equalizer.

Are you still drinking oat water? *(I'd told Bill about bodybuilder Bill Pearl's unique remedy for damaged muscles.)*

Yeah. I get steel cut oats from the health food store. I put about a cup in a pot and pour on boiling water. I let it sit overnight and drink it in the morning. It promotes fast healing. People might laugh, but it works. Products in the oats release the natural cortisone in the body. And that helps the healing process. It tastes lousy at first, but if you mix it with apple juice or lemon, it's not bad.

What kind of weight training do your players at Cal do?

We're very big on free weights. Right now though, we're going through an 18-station isokinetic workout. They're machines based on a set resistance. You get a great workout in 35 minutes. Nort Thornton, the

Videos by Howard Gutstadt

Jack Fulton

Bill Wright and the contents of his sports-minded van

Cal swimming coach (see p. 118) started it.

So the correlation between playing winning tennis and fitness is on the players' minds these days..

Oh, yeah. Tennis is in a fitness phase right now. People are seeing how great Martina Navratilova is playing. She is a real product of the technical fitness era. She runs, lifts weights and really watches her diet. And Chris Evert Lloyd, just to keep up, has to follow suit.

Haas's book, *Eat to Win,* has had a tremendous effect on athletes. People have a long-range philosophy about diet now. Habits have changed for good. The Haas book and Pritikin are the reason.

The most important thing is to do something every day. It doesn't have to be tennis, it doesn't have to be weights. Anything to get moving and get a sweat up is great.

A common complaint about tennis has been, "We don't get a good enough workout." Now, players take an hour they might have spent goofing around with their serve to go to an aerobics class. The serious players are spending more thought and time trying to get fit because they know it helps them play better. □

Dick Zanuck

Dick Zanuck and I were roommates at Stanford in the mid '50s. About every other week we'd take off for L.A., driving all night so we could spend the weekend surfing at Malibu and playing volleyball on the beach. We made surfing safaris to Baja in a 20th Century Fox jeep and were about the second surfers to go to Mazatlan (in 1954). Zanuck was a great volleyball player and a fierce competitor. We'd only been in touch a few times since college and when we talked recently, discovered we were both running, swimming and found working out to be a crucial part of each day's schedule. He had just run in the New York Marathon and I was getting ready for my first one. I met him at his house on the beach in Santa Monica at 6 A.M. one weekday morning and we took off on his usual 5-mile run through the streets. Then we came back and jumped in the ocean for a swim.

After college Zanuck went directly to work in the movie business and at age 34 became president of 20th Century Fox–then the youngest corporate head of any studio. At Fox he was in charge of production of Butch Cassidy and the Sundance Kid, M*A*S*H, Patton *and* The French Connection. *After a blowup with Fox in the early '70s he teamed up with David Brown to form Zanuck-Brown productions. Among their films have been* The Sting, Jaws, The Verdict, *and* Cocoon.

Zanuck set a 100-yard butterfly swimming record in high school, now runs and swims almost every morning, and works on weight machines three days a week. Now 51, he plays tennis, skis about 30 days a year and occasionally gets thrown in jail for running with his dogs on the Santa Monica Beach.

Vital Statistics

Dick Zanuck, 51
Date of Birth: December 13, 1934
Born: Los Angeles, California
Height: 5'6" **Weight:** 137
Job: Film producer
Lives in: Santa Monica, California
Activities: Running, swimming, tennis, skiing

How long have you been running?

About 10 or 12 years.

Do you run every day?

Yeah. All year long at 5:30 A.M. I can't sleep any longer. I do some abdominal exercises, just leg raises, some pushups and some stretches. Then I'll run 5 miles, come back home and jump in the ocean. If I have time I'll swim between lifeguard stations *(about 250 yards)*, especially when the water gets a little warmer. But during the cold months I'll just go in and out. Then I'll shower and go to work.

Three times a week a guy comes over and we work out on this Marcy Gym, and also do this inversion thing where you hang upside down. It takes about an hour.

How much sleep do you get a night?

About 6 hours. That's about it . . . .

You ran the '82 New York Marathon?

Yeah.

How fast?

3:30

What did you do to train for the marathon?

I started about 2½ months ahead of time–10 weeks. I mean seriously training for it. I did about 70-80 miles a week. But towards the end, I did a 20 instead of the 10 and then a week later, I did another 20.

What about dietary changes?

I stopped drinking entirely–you know, not even a beer, not even a Coca Cola or a Tab, no coffee.

When you get further and further out the thought process is amazing. The clarity of your thinking. There's a rhythmic flow of your whole body, heart and everything else.

Before that I used to have a few drinks every night. But when I started this program, I felt so good, I stuck with it.

What was the marathon like?

Everybody tells you not to start out too fast but no matter how many times you hear that you still do.

So you went out too fast, like 7½ minutes a mile?

7¼ to 7½, it must have been, because I averaged 8. I know I was really slowed down the last 5 miles. I started to stiffen up—just general exhaustion. You know, what they say is absolutely true. The race is divided into two parts, the first 20 and the last 6. The last 6 your body starts going into reserves—and they better be there. I didn't hit "the wall" and I didn't have to stop but I was pretty well shot—just total fatigue.

Are you going to try any other races?

Maybe. You know, it's not the race itself, it's all the preparation. I find myself taking it so seriously. When I was training for the marathon, I was doing at least 10 miles a day in the early morning. So I was running in total darkness. It was taking me 80 minutes on the run itself. So I had to get up earlier and everything was backed up.

Do you take problems out there to solve?

Yes. I find it very productive. It does two things—it solves problems because I can't sit in my office and just stare at a wall for 40 minutes and think about one subject—there are too many distractions; plus nobody has that kind of control unless you're a guru or something. But on the run you

Bob Seidemann

Dick running on beach in front of his home in Santa Monica, California

He pulled up and jumped out of his jeep and tackled me. Handcuffed me to the door of his jeep.

can zero in on one subject, select the subject before the run and just stay with it. It's amazing how thoroughly you can analyze a subject and come up with a problem-solving solution with 40 minutes of concentrated thought. No phone calls, no interference. It achieves two purposes. It helps you in your business, or you can concentrate on private or personal things. Like what I want to do with the boys, and it can range from far-reaching things about their future, or it can be what are they going to do this summer, or problems that I have with my daughters, anything like that. A lot of times I'll take a script idea with me and analyze it thoroughly to decide whether I want to take it on as a movie or not.

In your work now, do you read books and scripts? Do you have people that filter them out for you?

I read practically all of it myself and it's awfully time consuming. I read a couple of books and probably three or four scripts a week. Thinking about these things also takes some of the boredom and the hurt out of the run because you hardly know you've been running–you've had the physical pleasure of the run but your mind has been on something else. So you don't think, "Oh my Achilles hurts, my knee hurts, my back hurts." It's a good device for me. It's the only activity I can think of where you can spend that much concentrated thought on one subject for that long a time. It's a great form of meditation.

They say that after 30 minutes of running the oxygen gets to your brain.

Yes, when you get further and further out the thought process is amazing. The clarity of your thinking. There's a rhythmic flow of your whole body, heart and everything else.

What about when you did *The Sting* or *Jaws* and things got very successful in your business. Did running help keep you focused?

Through good and bad times, the running has remained pretty constant. In fact during bad times I find myself running more and farther. Maybe it's kind of an escape.

Instead of going to a shrink or something?

Yeah, I know when I left Fox in all that furor and I didn't have a job or anything and I didn't know what I was going to do, whether I was going to make pictures for myself or go with another studio, I found myself asking all the probing questions on those long runs and I was able to think through problems in a clear state of mind.

What do you do when you travel? When you went to the Cannes Film Festival, were you able to run?

I didn't miss a day. I only missed one day and I made it up when I got home. That's the great thing about running, you don't need a lot of equipment, just a pair of shoes and shorts. I've run wherever I've been, whether it's Tokyo or Vienna. I run up at Sun Valley after skiing.

Do you travel a lot?

Well, most of the films I've made have been away from town. *The Verdict* was made in Boston and New York. I stayed there the whole time. When we made *Jaws,* I was on Martha's Vineyard for 5 months.

You guys do a film a year or something?

Yeah, I've got a spy adventure story that takes place in Munich. I'm putting that together. I'll be in Japan, I'll be in New York, I'll be in Munich, I'll be in Florida. And I always like to get in 25 or 30 days of skiing every year. I like to get in a couple of trips to the Islands.

I heard you had a little trouble with the law over running with your dogs on the beach. What was that?

I had these two Staffordshire bull terriers and they ran with me every morning. There's a law against dogs on the beach and I ended up with 20 tickets. The dogs loved it so much and I didn't see any harm in it. I'd go out at 5:30 in the morning and nobody was out there. But the dog catcher invariably would get me.

So he threw you in jail?

Yeah, because I got so pissed off. I guess I was about a mile from my house the last time and the guy pulled up in his jeep and started writing out a ticket, so I said, "Oh fuck this," and I took off. He had to get back in his jeep. *(Laughter)* He couldn't keep up with me in his boots, you know, and I was trying to work my way back to the house. But then I got into the heavy sand and I was slowed down. He pulled up and jumped out of his jeep and tackled me. Handcuffed me to the door of his jeep. *(Laughter)* He then radioed and they put me in a paddy wagon, took me up to Santa Monica jail and put me in a cell. I got out of it right away, but you know . . . .

The perils of running.

Yeah. □

OVER THE HILL is the first in a series of books to be published every few years about people past 40 who keep in shape. Do you know of anyone with an interesting story to tell? What are *you* doing these days? Please write or call us if you have stories, information or ideas to share.

Shelter Publications, Inc.
PO Box 279
Bolinas CA 94924
415/868-0280

Remember: Once you're over the hill, you pick up speed . . .